Personal Sociology

Personal Sociology

Finding Meanings
in Everyday Life

Jeffrey E. Nash

LEXINGTON BOOKS
Lanham • Boulder • New York • London

Published by Lexington Books
An imprint of The Rowman & Littlefield Publishing Group, Inc.
4501 Forbes Boulevard, Suite 200, Lanham, Maryland 20706
www.rowman.com

86-90 Paul Street, London EC2A 4NE

Chapter 1: Parts of this chapter were previously published in Journal of Contemporary Ethnography. 2012. Vol. 41: 581-606.
Chapter 3: Parts of this chapter were previously published in Qualitative Sociological Review. 2021. XVII (2): 88-102.
Chapter 4: Parts of this chapter were previously published in Studies in Symbolic Interaction. 2008. Vol. 32: 183-198.
Chapter 5: Parts of this chapter were previously published in Michigan Journal of Sociology 2020. Vol 34 (Fall): 106-128.
Chapter 8: Parts of this chapter were previously published in the Arkansas Democrat-Gazette and are used with permission. Copyright © 2022 by The Rowman & Littlefield Publishing Group, Inc.

British Library Cataloguing in Publication Information Available

Library of Congress Cataloging-in-Publication Data

Names: Nash, Jeffrey E., author.
Title: Personal sociology : finding meanings in everyday life / Jeffrey E. Nash.
Description: Lanham : Lexington Books, [2022] | Includes bibliographical references and index. | Summary: "In Personal Sociology, Jeffrey E. Nash transforms everyday experiences into sociological insights and understandings. Through eight chapters in three thematic sections, personal sociology is illustrated by the author's reflections on activities from his own life that expand these particular experiences into broader sociological concepts"— Provided by publisher.
Identifiers: LCCN 2021051298 (print) | LCCN 2021051299 (ebook) | ISBN 9781793651587 (cloth ; alk. paper) | ISBN 9781793651594 (ebook)
Subjects: LCSH: Sociology. | Applied sociology.
Classification: LCC HM585 .N38 2022 (print) | LCC HM585 (ebook) | DDC 301—dc23/eng/20211021
LC record available at https://lccn.loc.gov/2021051298
LC ebook record available at https://lccn.loc.gov/2021051299

Contents

Contents

List of Figures and Tables

FIGURES

TABLES

Acknowledgments

The chapters in this book acknowledge the people whose lives make up the content of the book. They accepted me as a friend, co-participant, or as a detached observer of whatever was going on. The people whose academic work and thought influenced me are present in the text as well. Charles Tolbert encouraged and supported me when I was an undergraduate at Baylor University. Then, at Louisiana State, Joe Perry suggested that I study with Dick Ogles at Washington State. My tenure at Macalester College allowed me to learn from Jim Spradley and Dave McCurdy. Thanks to them, I became a closet anthropologist. John Johnson and Paul Higgins's early anthology of personal sociology obviously had a lasting effect on my sociology.

To all my barbershop singing buddies from the Show-Me Statesmen, the Diamond State Chorus (A Cappella Rising), and the Greater Ozark Chorus, I owe gratitude for the emotional attachments I have for them, especially for the rollicking good times had with fellow tenor, Marc Carter. And the coaches and kids of the wrestling world welcomed me. Thanks to the coach who let me work out with his high school team, and a big thanks to the coach who ran the program at the 7th Street Salvation Army gym in St. Paul, Minnesota.

I should thank the medical staff at University of Arkansas Medical Sciences for my technologically enhanced penis. Thanks to the nurses and to Dr. Delk. Without that surgery, there could be no chapter Three.

Norm Denzin encouraged me to dive deep into television when I submitted my article on the sitcoms to him. He went beyond editorial suggestions to introduce me to a rich literature on humor and television. The folks at the life-long learning program, Life Quest, allowed me to teach and learn from them and share a few laughs.

Anne Sutherland introduced me to anthropological literature on animals and the classes we taught together at Macalester on animal human relationships inform chapter Seven. To the people who struggled to stop the construction of the Turk coal plant, I encourage to be brave and keep fighting. Maybe what we learned about how people think about the environment can somehow help with the cause.

To Dina Nash, my wife and coauthor of chapter Seven, I offer a special acknowledgment. Without her, this project would have been doomed from the start. She read, made suggestions, and generally made this book possible—all done with care and love. Thanks, Dina.

Introduction

Discovering Sociology

In most sociological research, the sociologist is absent. There are exceptions which I discuss later in this chapter. In personal sociology, the sociologist is at the center of the research. He or she becomes the focal point from which observations and analysis flow. The essays in this collection emanate from my involvement in social scenes and my real-life experiences. Personal sociology reveals aspects of the sociologist as a person. This volume is not a memoir because too much is left out. However, some background might be helpful for understanding how these essays constitute personal sociology.

Both my mother and father were high school graduates—Dad from Tulsa Central High in 1936 and Mom from Cleveland, Oklahoma, high school in 1934. While Dad attended the University of Tulsa for one semester, that was about the extent of formal education that made up the learning environment I grew up in. There was no library in our home. *Life* magazine, *Reader's Digest* and the local conservative newspaper, the *Tulsa Tribune*, were sources of information. I think the family might have subscribed to *National Geographic*—at least I remember issues of it because of the pictures of bare-breasted native women from somewhere exotic.

We were not really poor. Dad worked at the local oil refinery where his dad had been employed as a sheet metal worker. During the Great Depression my grandfather, who died before I was born, never lost his job. And my dad was working at the same refinery as a time-keeper when I was young. He later moved up into an accounting job and finally received training, at company expense, to create the first online fueling station where tanker trucks were filled with gasoline.

I mention this aspect of my personal story because it relates to my working-class, lower-middle-class background. My next revelation, not surprisingly, is about my religious upbringing. We were Southern Baptists. When I was

1

young my father refused to attend the church that my mother took us to. Mom didn't learn to drive until she was in her forties: she would have Dad drive her, my sister, and me to church. Dad would pick us up after the service. Our church was evangelical, so there were still amens and a little shouting of praise when the preacher made a point that resonated with the congregation's beliefs. I remember being a little embarrassed when this happened. I was friends with pastor Brother Wade's son, Jimmy, who was a preacher's kid—fun loving and a bit rowdy. We would often skip Sunday school and roam the church's out-of-way places, even running on the roof from building to building.

Jimmy and I, as 12-year-old boys, were not that affected by sermons and altar calls (referred to as invitations in Southern Baptist circles). But the messages of salvation in lieu of eternal damnation did get through to me. I remember vividly the Sunday morning when I "heard" the call and responded. I professed my belief in Jesus Christ as my personal Lord and savior, and I felt thereafter no longer in the grave danger of burning in hell.

I don't remember what my dad thought of this, or my mom for that matter, and with more than six decades of hindsight, I can see that my profession of faith was far from genuine. The first harbinger of trouble with faith came when I was baptized. All Baptist churches are built with a bathtub-like fixture, usually behind the choir, which is filled with water—three-and-a-half feet or so. The preacher may wear wading boots and the folks to be dunked wear robes. Well, these robes were thin and white. Women and girls entered the baptismal from one side, men and boys and men from the other. When I was "on deck," you might say, a woman was in the water with Brother Wade. When she emerged from the water, her white robe clung to her skin and she was not wearing a bra. So, when I waded in the water for the declaration of my faith, I saw a wet tee-shirt show of ample breasts—a sensuous image anchored in my long-term memory.

Well, I was 12 years old and high school lay ahead. My dad finally agreed to attend church, but only if we stepped up to the First Baptist church downtown. It was a farther drive but definitely upwardly mobile: the building was grand, the sanctuary looked sacred, and the members were more likely to be college-educated and professional than those of my mother's choice of worship.

Throughout high school, I was a religious guy. I never did proselytize but while a member of a social club and an athlete, I walked the straight and narrow. And at age 16, I heard another call: this time to be a preacher. I met with the governing body of the church. They asked me a few questions about how I knew I was supposed be man of God. I don't recall my answers, other than they were honest. I must have conjured up some convincing words, because they agreed that I had heard the call, and I was granted a preacher's license.

The license didn't mean much except that I could qualify for a slight discount on tuition at a Baptist university or college. The men of my church suggested that I attend Oklahoma Baptist College. My dad drove me to visit the campus and, as a city kid, I could not image attending there. So, we settled on Baylor University, a fortuitous decision for unanticipated reasons. My time as a pre-ministerial student lasted three semesters. The Biblical studies classes I took fascinated me because of something the professors called "critical analysis." It seemed, so they said, that the appropriate way to understand the Bible was to search for the cultural and historical context in which the text was composed. "What? I thought the Bible was the literal word of God. How could that be influenced by what people were doing?"

But I thrived in these classes, and, in hindsight, they fueled what shortly was to become my sociological vocation. In my second year as a pre-ministerial student, I was required to take a course in the history of the Southern Baptist church. I was bewildered by the claim that Baptists were not a part of the Protestant reformation. I could sense a thinly veiled anti-Catholic bias, and the approach this class took, to my young mind, contradicted the critical analysis that so enthralled me. My faith in my calling to be a Baptist minister was fading, along with my tolerance for all the praying my roommate insisted upon. Finally, it couldn't bear it anymore; I forfeited the tuition credit, went secular, and got a new roommate.

Then, as a junior, I took my first sociology class. At Baylor in the 1960s, junior status was a prerequisite for taking any sociology class. Apparently, the curriculum prerequisites were supposed to warn naive students of the heretical nature of the sociological imagination. Sociology was heretical for me, at least in the sense that Peter Berger suggested in *Rumor of Angels*. Berger sets the task of believing in religion and the transcendental against the rationality of the modernization process. As a young undergraduate in search of a way to understand the complexity of belief systems, I took comfort in Durkheim's observation that God is made in the image of man, that is, that human understandings of God are shaped by social facts. I remember giving a presentation on Durkheim's *Elementary Forms of Religious Life* in a senior seminar that was held in the conference room of Tidwell Bible Building, which we sociology majors called the Tidwell Tower of Power. Somehow a sociological account of religion made more sense to me than the tropes of religion, tropes that I learned mirror the social facts of a given society and culture. I excelled in the classroom and attracted the attention of the faculty, particularly Charles Tolbert who was department chair. As a senior I was working for the department grading papers and assisting faculty with their classes. My second call ended with an abrupt "wrong number."

The third call led to the person I was becoming and to my lifelong career. I still attended Sunday school in those days, and I remember after I gave a talk about something, the Sunday school teacher said to me, "You sound like a sociologist." Whether this was an insult or a compliment, I'll never know, but I took as a compliment.

The clarion call of sociology led me to graduate school at Louisiana State University where I finished my master's degree in one year—eager to have my calling certified. From the heat and humidity of Louisiana, I headed to the great Palouse country of eastern Washington State to continue my studies toward the PhD. However, I was drafted into the US Army, interrupting my doctoral work. Most of my term of duty was served as a company clerk for the administrative company for the 2nd Armored Division (Hell on Wheels), stationed at Fort Hood, Texas.

I clerked from a Weberian perspective (from inside the iron cage), which to me was an awareness of the alienation and fragmentation of emotions, so that my primary concern was with muddling through to survive. While the threat of being sent to Vietnam was ever-present, I coped with the distinction between the formal and informal structures of complex organizations. In this case, that involved the "going on leave" game in which soldiers would ask me to leave them off the morning report so that they could receive pay for unused leave days when they mustered out of active-duty service. Of course, this was a violation of Army regulations and could have resulted in serious consequences, which was nerve-wracking.

While I was ethically conflicted when I took over from the previous clerk who had developed a fairly lucrative business from the practice, I recognized that if I chose to "blow the whistle" on this clerk, I would disrupt this informal practice, much to my detriment. For example, fellow draftees also bent on avoiding being sent to Vietnam, actually "cut the orders" for Vietnam, and they were known to retaliate against those who did not "play along" with the scheme by including their names on the orders. Since I was opposed to the war, along with most of the draftees who worked as clerks of various sorts in the administration company, I wanted to stay on the good side of these men. Hence, when they asked me to hide their leave days, I did so, but I never took money for it, which further endeared me to them.

I am not sure I would have understood the complexity of this informal system without my sociological imagination. This practice of hiding leave by omitting departure and return days from the morning report which was the official record of the whereabouts of all 500 men in the company was so widespread that it was overlooked by an inspector from the 4th Army who conducted annual inspections of the company records. And after having been clerk for sixteen months serving with the same first sergeant, I relaxed a bit when this career soldier who had been Elvis Presley's drill sergeant came to my desk one day and told me he was going on leave and winked at me knowingly, anticipating that I got the message and would hide his leave days.

One of the happiest days of my life was getting out the Army and returning to WSU to finish my PhD. The pressures of graduate school paled in comparison to the tight rope I had walked in the Army. Having learned about bureaucracy and living in the iron cage of rationality, I understood how to survive two years as a draftee.

I returned to graduate school in a climate of unrest as the Vietnam War continued and student activism was at a peak. I was focused on following my calling to sociology. While I supported many of the goals of student activists, I wanted to finish my studies and move on to a life as a professional sociologist. I taught classes as part of my teaching assistantship and I passed my doctoral preliminary examinations.

My first wife and I adopted a Native American baby during this time who happened to be deaf. Learning to communicate with my new son stimulated a keen interest in understanding the experiences of deaf people. I wanted to do my dissertation on parents of deaf children, but I discovered that project would entail travel to Spokane and an elaborate permission process to gain access to parents through the public schools. So, I accepted an offer by my officemate to share a data set he and his advisor had collected from a state-wide survey. That survey included the Twenty Statements Test. I did a linguistic analysis of the sentences that respondents wrote and correlated indicators of syntactic complexity with those of various self-appraisals. I found that people who wrote long, complex sentences were less self-affirming than those who wrote short, simple ones: hardly a profound discovery, but it was sufficient for a dissertation and a few journal publications.

This was a long way from understanding sign language and the Deaf community. I postponed that endeavor, returning to it years later. Still, I was on a vocational track, which I understood in a Weberian sense as referring to the practice of systematic self-control in the pursuit of goals or purposes. The concept of calling (*Beruf*) identifies what is required to realize in action the quality of rationality, even with the support of emotions (Weber 1946). I moved to my first academic job with a passion for doing sociology.

The Spradley Connection

My first tenure-track sociology teaching employment was at the University of Tulsa. This was a homecoming of sorts, since I had been away for a decade. I think my parents were proud of me for landing the position, but I was never sure, since I had become a "secular humanist" (a liberal college sociology professor), while my father had immersed himself in conservative social networks, having become the Worshipful Master of a large Masonic Lodge in Tulsa.

A turn of events brought my major PhD adviser, Richard H. Ogles, from Washington State, to Tulsa as a full professor, along with a mutual colleague. We shared academic perspectives, and I was successfully publishing articles derived from my dissertation. Tragedy soon appeared in the return of my dad's colon cancer. His declining health began within six months of my arrival in Tulsa, and that episode of my life became sorrowful. Although my graduate training was decidedly quantitative, I had developed an interest in sociolinguistics and qualitative research. I am not sure how I came across the work of James Spradley; perhaps it was through a mutual interest in deafness (his brother had a deaf daughter and I, a deaf son). I was drawn to the systematic way that he described cultural knowledge. His taxonomic analysis of the experiences of tramps in *You Owe Yourself a Drunk* fascinated me. I even envisioned his approach as illustrative of collective consciousness, a social reality larger than the sum of the parts. Through Spradley's approach, collective reality became vivid and visible.

I invited Spradley to visit Tulsa and give a lecture on his methods. He declined, but I pressed on. After several attempts, he agreed. He gave the lecture, and he and I hit it off. He informed me that his department at Macalester College was hiring. The department included sociology and anthropology (throughout my career, I have worked in combined departments), and the three anthropologists were looking for a sociologist whose research and perspective were consistent with cultural analysis. By this time, I had become deeply interested in qualitative sociology (ethnomethodology and symbolic interaction), and I had just published "Community on Wheels," which was a participant observation study of riding a city bus. To me, the underlying principle in qualitative analysis was linguistic. Interaction and social realities themselves were products of talking and using language.

I applied for the position, was hired, and began a 20-year career at Macalester College, where I was able to pursue my study of deaf people and their language and community. I learned a lot from Jim Spradley. He taught several of us his approaches to interviewing, participant observation, and the use of life histories as techniques for the description and understanding of cultural knowledge and action. His much-too-short life ended at 48 years of age, but my work and, in particular my personal sociology, has been indelibly shaped by my relationship with James P. Spradley (Nash and McCurdy 1990). I moved from Macalester to Missouri State, and finally to the University of Arkansas at Little Rock. My career consists of experience at liberal arts colleges and state universities.

At this point, my journey has been both similar and distinctive from those found in *Journeys in Sociology: From First Encounters to Fulfilling Retirements* (Darling and Stein 2017). In that anthology, retired sociologists briefly recount how they came to the discipline and the directions their careers took. The accounts are organized by generation, but in the introduction, Darling (Darling and Stein 2017, 3–4) relates that notable themes did appear in the journeys. Some simply bumped into sociology on their way to somewhere else. Earl Babbie called himself an "accidental sociologist," and Bob Perrucci stayed in college and "discovered" sociology through the suggestion of a friend.

With very few exceptions (perhaps Alice Goffman or Charles Tolbert III), most of us as children did not envision becoming a sociologist as a child might think of herself as becoming a doctor, a firefighter, or a "cop." In a sense, all sociologists find the discipline. But for other authors in *Journeys,* sociology was a choice derived from their social activism. Still others imagined themselves as "outsiders" and found in sociology a way to understand their life histories. And, then, there are accounts of finding sociology as a way to deal with early experiences of inequality, poverty, or discrimination.

The paths to becoming a professional sociologist are varied. And, of course, choices are always personal, in that they are shaped by socialization, social structures, and culture. Even the specialty within sociology and one's choice of topics to research are personal. The study of disability, for example, is often conducted by those with a disability or by the able-bodied who have a personal, often imitate relationship with a disabled person.

My Personal Sociology

I contend that all journeys to sociology, whether accidental, anchored in being an outsider, or rooted in esoteric personal experience, are personal in the sense that the sociologist can be recognized in the sociology. But the connection between the personal and professional is often tacit or intentionally hidden. What I wish to demonstrate is that personal experiences can be the evidence for sociological accounts and even theories that explain societal phenomena. Personal experiences serve as the sociological foundation for the study of social phenomena. My personal sociology emanates from a calling, a life-long commitment to the application of the sociological imagination to life experiences.

My calling has persisted for 50 years, and, in hindsight, I can see that my own experiences have been embedded in the way I have practiced sociology. I recall a colleague saying that I was the only sociologist he knew who turned virtually every personal experience into a scholarly paper. He had a point. Here are a few examples.

When our adopted deaf son was an infant, I recorded his language development while using cued speech; then after that I shifted him to Sign Language, recording his language development using signs in the same manner. Using my data, I published a scholarly article, ("Cues or Signs: A Case Study in Language Acquisition" in *Sign Language Studies*, 1973), showing that language acquisition through Sign Language followed patterns recognized by researchers, while language learning via cued speech did not. In other words, when my wife and I shifted from cued speech to signs, our son began acquiring language naturally. This study revealed our personal aspirations for our son to have communicative competency and was the beginning of my research in the Deaf community.

As my involvement with the Deaf community increased and we had a TTY machine in our home, I collected the paper documents of typed conversations. Also, with permission, I got scripts of conversations from a large department store, and I published an analysis of how conversations are conducted on TTYs ("Typing on the Phone: How the Deaf Accomplish TTY Conversations," *Sign Language Studies* 1984). I rode the bus to work and wrote "Bus Riding: Community on Wheels" (*Urban Life* 1974). I took up running for exercise and became involved in the running community in the Twin Cities and used my personal experiences to write several articles ("Lying About Running: The Functions of Talk in a Scene," *Qualitative Sociology* 1981 and "Weekend Racing: Understanding the Accomplishment of Well Being," *Urban Life* 1980).

Even the birth of my second son became grist for the sociological mill ("Conflicting Interpretations of Childbirth: The Medical and the Natural Perspectives," *Urban Life* 1979). When my family camped out in the Rocky Mountains for two summers, I collected observations on how territory can be marked ("The Family Camps Out: A Study in Nonverbal Communication," *Semiotica* 1984), and when my family bought an English Bulldog, that became an opportunity to apply a sociological perspective to animals ("What's in a Face? The Social Character of the English Bulldog," *Qualitative Sociology* 1989). In this book I present more examples of my personal sociology. Of course, I am not the first or the only sociologist to use personal experiences as evidence.

The idea of "personal sociology" has been implicit in the vocational call that some say led them to become professional sociologists. The idea is that the invitation to sociology implies passionate examination of the ordinary circumstances of one's own life, using opportunities that emerge in everyday life as "researchable" experiences. Berger acknowledged how difficult it might be to compartmentalize a sociological understanding from a personal one.

The sociologist lives in society, on the job and off it. His own life, inevitably, is part of his subject matter. Men [sic] being what they are, sociologists too manage to segregate their professional insights from their everyday affairs. But it is a rather difficult feat to perform in good faith. (Berger 1963)

So how about just using personal experiences as evidence for sociological insights? This is exactly what personal sociology does, and there are many examples, although they were not always identified as personal sociology. Roth (1963) turned his tuberculosis into opportunities to test sociological concepts. Roy (1952) used his job in a machine shop to create evidence for generalizations about how workers organized their time on the line. And more recently, the term personal sociology was used by Higgins and Johnson (1988) to refer to a collection of papers on topics such as youth sports, learning roles in the Navy, playing poker, growing up in a ghetto, being a victim of spousal abuse, working as an electrician, a caretaker, and a political activist.

Higgins suggests that personal sociology weds our lives with the study of social life. It is reflexive, requiring that we develop a keen awareness of our part in the making of the social worlds we act in. He reminds us that while our experiences are personal, they are not individualistic. Our lives are embedded in the lives of others, both in our immediate grasp and beyond, to our imagined shared histories. Personal sociology, de facto, reflects our concerns and worries, our hopes and fears for ourselves and those with whom we interact. Sociology that emanates from personal social life is a concerned sociology, one that promotes engagement and involvement in social life. Perhaps it is limited to the scope of one's experiences but nevertheless illuminating concerns about health, well-being, and even the future of people on earth.

Higgins's *How Was School Today: A Father and Daughter's School-Year Journey* (2004) is a description of the conversations he had with his fifth-grade daughter about what happened at school each day for an entire school year. He recorded these conversations and recounted them in the book. They portray the school experience from the daughter's point of view and provide insights into the children, the school, even the father. Higgins notes that children's experiences are rich and under appreciated, that children interpret what is happening to them in terms of past experiences and future expectations, that children often take parents and teachers more seriously than either the parent or the teacher realize. The images of children have of school often surprise the listener, for example, that even in small schools, peer interactions may be constrained, and the girl-boy interaction can be quite sophisticated among fifth graders. His observation about the importance of ritual and mitigating invidious comparisons among the children point to the potential for deeper knowledge that parents have of their children and that children have of their parents. All this is personal sociology.

Another example of a sociology of deeply personal experience is Anderson's *The Cosmopolitan Canopy* (2011). He writes:

> Engaged as a citizen as well as a disciplined sociologist, I have partaken of the broad spectrum of social life, becoming an "observing participant" . . . This

account conveys what I have seen and heard and presents what sense I have been able to make of interactions occurring in public. (xv–xvi)

From his personal view, Anderson writes of the shocking and revelatory experience that every African American recognizes at some time in their interactions with white folks. From racial profiling to talk around the office water cooler, there is often an occurrence which dramatically defines experience as racial. What Anderson defines as the "nigger moment" is the point in an otherwise civil interaction, when a person is reminded of "their putative place as a black person" (253). Reading the chapter of his book devoted to this experience starkly impresses the reality of these moments on the reader. Anderson's examples include an aggressive police search of a law student waiting for a bus and his being mistaken for a killer because of a description given to 911 by neighbors, and his humiliation as police treat him as a dangerous murder suspect; a mother's answer of a son's question "Why do black kids start all the trouble in school?"; and a young black man's comparing the number of times he has been pulled over by police to those of his white colleagues in the courses of casual conversation. From the seemingly trivial to the downright dangerous, racial identity seems inescapable, and reading these accounts, one cannot evade the realization that Anderson has lived that moment.

Doing personal sociology in a university setting can be problematic. Tenure committees may not want to consider credible articles based on personal sociology. And, of course, being awarded grant money to do personal sociology is rare, indeed. Furthermore, there is the troublesome matter of IRB's (boards to review research for standards of protection for subjects; often called Institutional Review Boards). Van Den Hoonaard's *The Seduction of Ethics* (2011) is perhaps the most careful analytic look at the misfit between the goals of ethical research on human subjects in the sciences and the goals of social science, particularly qualitative social science.

Bureaucratic policies based on common understandings of what is appropriate in research for universities have unintended consequences on social research. Van Den Hoonaard lists a few: hyperbolic claims about benefits of the research, homogenization of research methods, and the merger of disciplines. Each of these has a dampening effect on creativity. When getting approval from the IRB becomes a mandated step in conducting research, a researcher is reluctant to rock the boat with unusual and perhaps controversial topics and methods. Institutional Review Boards pressure researchers to be conservative in their projects, perhaps to the exclusion of innovative and controversial research.

Many research studies that still contribute form and substance to contemporary theories could not be conducted under the common rule that reigns today. For example, Humphreys's *Tea Room Trade,* Festinger, Riechkhen, and Schachter's *When Prophesy Fails*, or Muzafer Sherif's *Robbers Cave* natural experiment meets the minimal standards of informed consent: these researchers infiltrated without consent the groups they studied. Sherif, with parental consent, even manipulated children who attended a summer camp into assuming group identities for the purpose of testing hypotheses about group conflict and its resolution. At one point in the experiment, children carried canoes through a terrain which the boys thought was home to rattlesnakes. Humphreys recorded license plate numbers and traced these to the addresses of those he observed having sex in the tearooms. He later visited them to administer a survey about a topic seemingly unrelated to their sexual practices. The irony of *Tearoom* is that Humphreys himself was gay and that his study was designed to show, among other things, that these men were "normal" in their everyday life. Festinger deceived the people he was interviewing and his graduate students posed as believers and actually joined the cults being studied. No IRB would approve such studies today.

I suggest that personal sociology offers a way to conduct ethical research which can garner IRB approval while still providing creative space for novel analysis and theory. Here is my story of the research I conducted for chapter One of this volume. First, I must say that most of my career, and the research I conducted took place before the establishment of common rule committees like those that Van Den Hoonard studied, and my early participant observations were conducted at private institutions.

My first encounter with an IRB happened after I had retired and returned to a full-time academic appointment. I had been a member of two barbershop choruses when I began to think about interpreting my experiences sociologically. I had a completed manuscript which I submitted to the *Journal of Contemporary Ethnography*. The editors of the journal requested that I get IRB approval of the research before they would accept the paper. Now all the research had been completed, although I was still singing with a chorus and barbershop singing was, by now, a serious leisure time pursuit for me (Stebbins [2007], calls these pursuits "serious leisure"). Therefore, I was tasked with getting permission for something I had already done. I filled out all the necessary forms and, as you might guess, the forms were returned to me with some questions about informed consent. How could I procure consent from so many men and what would I ask them? Getting approval became a matter of educating the members of the IRB on the nature of some forms of qualitative research, particularly anthropological approaches the ethnography. I remembered that Jim Spradley once told me that his work consisted not of studying informants but learning from them. So, the people he interviewed and those his students used as informants were teachers, not subjects. This changed the ethics of "research" into one of personal responsibility and con-formity to the laws of slander and liable, as well as to ethical standards as laid out by professional associations such as the American Anthropological Society and the American Sociological Association, not IRBs.

I came up with another rationale for my barbershop study and pointed out that the rehearsals and shows, as well as other barbershop events, were pub-lic and therefore open to whatever evaluation an audience wished to make. I functioned, in effect, as an audience member and added to that my personal experiences. Since all observations were anonymous, and my study seemed to the members of the IRB to fit with guidelines for the study of public behavior, my project was approved. I was a student of barbershop and the men I learned from were my teachers.

Personal sociology predates autoethnography and tends to rely more on mainstream sociological concepts and perspectives than does autoethnogra-phy. Much of contemporary autoethnography seeks to merge artful expres-sions such as poetry and dramatic narratives, grounded in personal experi-ences, to create new insights related to broader cultural and societal trends (Adams, Ellis, and Jones 2017). Bochner and Ellis (2016) introduce a wide range of ways to write about personal experience. They call these approaches to narration evocative autoethnography which can include the creation of lit-erary forms, performative art, poetry, multi-voiced narration, dialogic forms, and co-constructed representations of lived experience.

While personal sociology may also be evocative, it differs in style and objectives, insisting that the "detached" stance of the observer be maintained, or at least attempted. Personal sociology is participant observation with an open mind to the reciprocal relationship between observation and personal experience. The essays in this book are closer to what Anderson calls analytic autoethnography (Anderson 2006) than they are to autoethnography.

Berger in his *Invitation to Sociology* points out that sociology as a dis-cipline has a foot in both the humanities and sciences. In the decades since *Invitation* much has changed, but his observation is still relevant. Autoeth-nography has moved toward the humanities, while the boundary between detached observation and creative expression has blurred to such a degree that sociological poetry and self-revelatory narratives become indistinguish-able from creative writing. On the other side of the continuum, economists have pushed their analysis into sociology with behavioral economics. Also, development of powerful nonlinear statistics programs capable of mining vast data banks has relegated qualitative analysis to the periphery of the discipline. Between the still-raging debates (see the roiling storm over Alice Goffman's *On the Run*) about the standards of inquiry, personal sociology has a place. Personal sociology claims a center position between the extremes of mathematical modeling and data mining and the subjectivity of autoethnography. The chapters in this book are grounded in my experiences, but they are presented as evidence for sociological interpretations. The topics emanate from my life world and are personal in that I am present in the analysis, but they are described and understood using sociological concepts and theories.

Each chapter of this book begins with a back story in which I tell about my personal involvement in a social scene. That involvement serves as evidence for the sociological perspectives I develop. For instance, how do male singers with ordinary families and jobs who are required daily to be stoic and reserved manage to become so sentimental and effusive about preservation and performance of a music genre? I am a barbershop singer and I puzzle over this question in my own life. In another study I pose the questions, "How do people discuss global warming in ways that reflect who they are and what they do? What sense does resistance to the construction of a coal plant make for those who campaign against coal-fired production of electricity?" In that study, I write from the perspective of a social activist who tried, unsuccessfully, to stop the construction of a 600-megawatt coal plant in a pristine region of southwest Arkansas.

Other questions I have addressed in my work on race are these: "How do we understand the way people talk about race? Is there a portrait of this kind of talk in mass media that reveal changes and shifts in discourse? Can being a fan of Larry David provide cues about racial narratives?" I show how the narratives of race in two TV programs separated by over 30 years reveal how race relationships have changed. My love of laughter and my interest in being funny motivated my analysis of the social aspects of humor, and the onset of impotence led to my understanding of how a medical procedure such as a penile implant can become naturally embodied in one's sense of self.

Each chapter stands as an independent analysis of a topic, but they build on participant observation in the social domain being described. They are therefore linked together through personal experience, and often they emanate from a commitment to some aspects of the experiences related; for example, from attempting to stop the construction of a coal plant, to promoting an often-neglected sport such as wrestling, and to appreciating a style of American singing.

I organize these chapters in parts. Each part presents essays that deal with the intersection of identities. For example, Part One, chapters One, Two, and Three, addresses how the meanings of gender are intertwined with other identities such as class and politics in singing barbershop style a cappella music, in competitive wrestling, and in the deeply personal experience of undergoing a penile implant operation. Part Two, chapters Four and Five, draw out the interconnections among humor, race, class, disability, and gender. Chapter Five demonstrates that teaching may provide a means to explicate these intersections. Chapter Four compares TV sit-coms' portrayal of race and class over a thirty-year period, revealing a dramatic change from modern and postmodern meanings. Part Three, chapters Six, Seven, and Eight, highlights how deeply embedded activism is in social contexts which are invariably local. Animal rights, abortion, and environmental issues intersect with gender, class, and location, and these chapters seek to uncover the resulting meanings.

Part I

The activities that people engage in are extensions and incubators of their identities. Participation in leisure time activities, the influence of intense engagement in a sport, and experiences in private life itself make up situations of interaction in which identities form, interact, and change. These strategic situations often reveal meanings that are the result of intersectionality. Only a few decades ago, this term was an obscure reference to a legal argument designed to show how discrimination can result indirectly from the coming together of several identities. Today the term is used to suggest that identities crisscross and intermingle to form novel meanings, emotions, and action.

The chapters in Part One illustrate intersectionality. When men sing together and ring the barbershop chord, they create and enact identities and emotions that are meaningful to them. They can express themselves emotionally in ways not possible in other aspects of their lives. When young boys and girls, with the support of their families and peers, wrestle in tournaments on Saturday afternoons, they are shaping identities that become part of their social selves. For the boys, their masculinity reflects the values of the sport, and girls alter the standards of toughness and fair play with their femininity.

Chapter Three depicts the details and complexity of having penile implant surgery and how the embodiment of the implant becomes a part of the intimate social self. The medical world and private habitus intersect to form new meanings for how the penis is understood and how a medicalized penis becomes a part of the social self.

Chapter One

Ringing the Chord

Sentimentality and Nostalgia Among Male Singers

I grew up listening to my father's barbershop quartet practicing in our dining room, sometimes into the late night.[1] This was in the 1950s, and efforts to organize, preserve, and encourage barbershop singing was only a decade old. Somehow those chords got through to me as I lay in my bed listening. Life went on and through many changes in my life, I retained an appreciation for that barbershop sound. But I never found the time of join a chorus or sing in a quartet. My dad died at 55 years of age, and I never got a chance to talk to him about his singing.

As I went through a very rough period of my life, I decided to start singing. I hunted down a local chorus, which took several attempts, and I began to sing. As I got to know my fellow singers, my sociological imagination led me to ask, "How do men, otherwise restrained by conventional masculinity, become so enamored with nostalgic and sentimental music?"

What do men accomplish when they devote significant portions of their leisure time to learning songs with sentimental lyrics, standing close to, singing in close harmony, and even dancing with other men? Is this hobby, called barbershop singing, at odds or congruent with members' sense of masculinity? Is emotional involvement with the sentimental music that characterizes barbershop singing outside the conventional template for manly activities? How do conservative ideas and gender intersect in the world of barbershop singing? These questions I explore through examining my own emotional experiences as a barbershop singer.

When I first visited a barbershop chorus chapter meeting, I was asked to stand in front of the chorus as a visitor. I did not know what to expect. The chorus, on the director's cue, sang to me: "You're as welcome as the flowers in May . . . Come along and sing your cares away." "Flowers in May?" I felt embarrassed and wondered what is going on here? This chorus comprised

17

of white, conservative, middle-aged men exhibited uncharacteristic warmth and openness. How can such obviously masculine men be so devoted to a leisure time activity that fosters the preservation of a form of music dripping with emotions of loss, sadness, grief, and, at the other end of the emotional continuum, joy, hope, and excitation? This musical hobby, so oddly and purposefully out of the mainstream, affords an opportunity to observe and understand masculine identity and expressivity. Through a thick description of the barbershop world, I characterize ways that conventional masculinity frames and expresses emotions, thereby adding depth to sociological understandings of the relationship between men's emotions and their gendered relationships.

MY METHOD: A LONG AND WINDING ROAD

My study is participatory and ethnographic (Spradley 1980). I rely extensively, however, on my personal experiences as a barbershop singer (Anderson 2006; Kleinman and Copp 1993). I am also opportunistic in that I take advance of naturally occurring events (Riemer 1977), and I am autoethnographic (Anderson 2006) in that I made purposeful attempts to interpret my own experiences conceptually.

My method for conducting research emerged from my immersion in the world of barbershop singing. For example, at particularly poignant moments when a chorus member revealed something personal, such as an illness or a family tragedy, I was both sympathetic and observant. I empathized, yet I remained analytic. For example, later in the paper, I analyze the way a chorus member turns his own divorce into a way of "feeling" the separation that the lyrics he is singing depict.

Autoethnography, as I employ the method, highlights the emotional aspects of everyday life settings (Dieser 2008). Recalling experiences, telling stories, and reflecting on what being a barbershopper means created opportunities to interpret "a culture or social group by producing highly personalized and revealing texts; it examines social phenomena holistically and underscores how social histories influence identity development" (Dieser 2008, 293–94).

Much of the descriptive information in this analysis consists of recollected or "delayed" observations. I preserve in my accounts and narratives both my feelings and thoughts in order to depict the world of barbershop singing. As Vasconcelos (2011) points out, autoethnography covers a wide variety of ways to convert autobiography into a method for doing research. She writes:

> Autoethnographers do not lose sight of their aim to explore and investigate the self. Since this research method makes room for various analytical lenses and understandings, the autoethnographic hybrid product can assume multifarious

shapes and scopes, on a continuum ranging from researchers sharing personal experiences with their respondents, which then become part of the larger research narrative, to wholly autobiographical projects, to those that explicitly combine autobiographical data and fiction. (Vasconcelos 2011, 417)

My autoethnography falls more on the analytic side of a continuum from self-revelation to analysis. I provide "observational evidence" for how the particular experiences of barbershoppers relate to larger concerns of understanding self in social context; in this case, the self is situated in emotional expressivity. Because I suspected that announcing that I am conducting research would alter the naturally occurring interaction among members, I conducted my research covertly, that is, as a regular chorus member (Lugosi 2006).

However, I have made no effort to conceal my desire to write about my experiences, and chorus members with whom I sing know that I am a sociologist. Furthermore, I have revealed to several chorus members that I have presented papers on barbershop singing at professional sociology meetings.

Documentation

To supplement my experiences and observations, I gathered printed materials on barbershopping, and I took extensive notes at workshops and sessions with judges who evaluated our chorus performances. After rehearsals, I wrote notes recording my reactions to things said, times when I laughed uncontrollably at jokes and gestures, and times when my feelings were hurt, when I was especially touched by the lyrics of a song, or the special way that song was performed. I attempted to record remarks *verbatim*, from recollection. I also collected several years of the Barbershop Harmony Society magazine, *The Harmonizer*, handouts from workshops, a small library of books about barbershop music, and a satchel full of sheet music.

My Journey

My personal motivation for joining such a group began with nostalgic memories of my father's quartet rehearsing in our family living room in Tulsa, Oklahoma. On my sixtieth birthday, for reasons I cannot fully recall, I decided to see if there was a barbershop chorus in my town. I had always found solace and comfort listening to ballads on the record album of the 1964 international quartet competition I purchased when I was an undergraduate student. Listening to that album constituted my main exposure to the barbershop world for more than thirty years. I did, however, sing in a calypso quartet in high school, and my father taught us one barbershop song, which we performed in a talent show.

While looking for a barbershop chorus to join, I ran across a badly out-of-date web page. After several unsuccessful attempts to find a rehearsal, I located two members of the local chorus. They invited me to visit their regular weekly rehearsal. A couple of rehearsals later, I was invited to audition with the chorus director, and I was asked to become a member of the chapter. Membership, it turns out, entailed more than learning, practicing, and performing music. Instead, it became a socialization process by which I eventually sounded and felt like a barbershopper.

Acquiring a Barbershop Habitus

Over the course of eight years, I became aware that I have acquired a barbershop habitus—a set of distinctive social, cognitive, and physical competencies associated with being part of social structures and organizations (Bourdieu 1984). Habitus, in this incidence, refers to "the practical sense," or the ability to function effectively within a given social field—knowing how, rather than knowing what (Lovell 2000, 27). Throughout this article, I rely on my habitus to produce realistic accounts of the barbershop experience. Because of my socialization, I can produce examples of verbal expressions, depict the details of chorus rehearsals, and reproduce the feelings of fellow barbershoppers (Agar 1996, Spradley 1980).

I began singing with a barbershop chorus to connect with memories of my father, to find a hobby that would allow escape from my ordinary routines, and to engage in an activity that I really enjoy, namely singing with men with whom I shared a passion for a particular style of music. After several years of participation, I became intrigued by my own emotional experiences, my reactions to singing sentimental songs, and my responses to expressing emotions through vocalization and gesturing.

When I decided to write about these experiences, I was instructed by an editor of a journal to secure approval from my local Institutional Review Board. I decided to ask for an exemption on the grounds that 1) that my work is observational, conducted in an open, public, impersonal setting; 2) members of choruses I sing with are aware that I am writing articles about barbershopping, and they are supportive of my efforts; and 3) my topics of study deal with abstract matters such as the sentimentality of the music and rituals of barbershop singing. Finally, 4) I gathered the observations I use following standard practices for conducting ethnographic research; that is, I use pseudonyms, disguise place and personal identities, and protect the confidentiality of my informants.

The first chorus I joined was in a Midwestern city where I was living, and after I moved from that location, I joined another chorus in the capital of a Southern state. I have traveled hundreds of miles to sing with my chorus in competition with other choruses. During rehearsals and performances. I have experienced a wide range of emotions from pride to embarrassment, and I have observed others experiencing and expressing strong feelings. While I intentionally avoided formal interviews with chorus members to maintain the "public and open" aspects of my observations, I have participated in hundreds of naturally occurring conversations about barbershop singing and performances.

In one chorus, I served as an officer, and in the other, as a board member, and in each chorus, I volunteered in several other supportive roles, such as putting up and taking down risers for rehearsals, selling tickets to performances, managing our annual scholarship competitions, or selling barbershop paraphernalia at district competitions.

Discovering Manly Singing

I set for myself an analytic task of understanding how conventionally masculine males could be preoccupied with sentimentality and nostalgia in this hobby, and how they bond without crossing into gay identities. In order to frame feelings and versions of the past in a masculine context, I turned to Kimmel (2006) who contends that as society changes, older versions of manhood are challenged, and new versions emerge. The new versions are often portrayed as aligned and consistent with the realities of existing social structure, in that they reflect changes in larger society such as employment patterns and trends in dating and marriage, while the older versions are seen as anachronistic, dissonant with the requirements of intimate relationships, and resistant to egalitarian societal trends (Anderson 2009).

According to the Kimmel (2008), men who resist change are often portrayed as remote, distant, angry, and potentially violent. Even the bonds that tie men together (masculine solidarity) are said to emerge from the crucibles of competition, sports teams (Messner 2002), the experience of combat (Hodgson 1999), and corporate liaisons (Beasley 2008). Hence, these ties are themselves potentially destructive, derisive of others, and emotionally flat (Connell 2005).

The men of the barbershop hobby are not destructive. They resist social change, however, especially in their choice to participate in an organization with the explicit goal of preserving an "out-of-date" musical form. And, from my discussions with wives and friends of barbershoppers, in their everyday lives these men were often, emotionally restrained, and curtailed (Scheff 1997). My assumptions about how they hid their emotions within conventional expression of masculinity seemed well founded. However, I began to see that masculinity might be expressed in many different forms and with varying contents (cf. Connell and Messerschmidt 2005).

The Christian Connection

Since approximately 80 percent of the men in the barbershop choruses that I studied are self-identified protestant Christians, I thought that understanding how conservative Christian versions of masculinity adapt to context might provide clues to understanding how barbershoppers think about manly singing. In their study of what counts as "manly" among conservative Christians, Gallagher, and Wood (2005) interviewed both men and women about what a male Christian should be according to their reading of a popular Christian book (*Wild at Heart* by John Elridge [2001]). They discovered that the slightly dangerous, aggressive, and adventuresome masculinity that the book advocates represents a revival of the older versions of the Christian self-made man. The *Wild at Heart* version of masculinity that the book presents is a reaction against "the rationalized nature of paid employment, as well as the responsible and 'feminized' expectations of Promise Keepers' ideal of servant leadership and involved fatherhood" (Gallagher and Wood 2005, 135).

Studies such as those of the conservative Promise Keeper's movement pertain to my experiences with barbershop singing since they reveal the complicated and resilient character of deeply held belief systems. These studies reveal conservative Christian movements to be, in large measure, attempts to maintain conventional meanings of masculinity in the face of profound changes in employment that threaten the central role of men as "bread winners" (Donovan 1998, Heath 2003). Furthermore, Gallagher and Smith (1999) illustrate that conservative men are willing to make changes in their lives on an interactional and personal level when these changes do not challenge the foundations of their sense of masculinity. They change, but they do not:

> grapple with the structural conditions that undergird their privilege. Their worldview follows from a tradition of American Evangelical Christianity that focuses on individuals rather than social structure. Concentrating on individual spirituality may not be a conscious attempt to maintain power. Yet the lack of attention to structural inequality does, in fact, reinforce existing power relations. (Heath 2003, 440)

Conservative men adapt to social change in many ways. For instance, in the pursuit of understanding underlying forces in antigay campaigns among conservative Christians, Stein (2005) shows that images of masculinity result in new forms of homophobia that are amalgams of traditional Christian beliefs and values and feminist criticisms. For example, Christian men may condemn blatant discrimination of gay people, yet hold tenaciously to values about the authority of men over their own families. Stein depicts the genesis of homophobias as evolving from resistance to challenges to traditional Christian beliefs and values about masculinity. Her research underscores the fluid nature of traditional images of masculinity, alongside the persistence of certain core attributes.

Mutable Masculinity

My survey of recent literature on masculinity suggests that interpretations of masculinity accommodate a wide range of variant meanings within the framework of "traditional masculinity" (Copes and Hochstetler 2003; Kaplan 2007; Leyser 2003; Schwalbe 1996). Core masculine values such as emotional detachment and patriarchic attitudes persist through and can even strengthen during participation in organizations and interactional settings that seem contradictory to these values. Conservative Christian men, it seems, adapt to threats to their world views in ways that allow them to maintain their foundational beliefs and continue to function in contemporary society.

As Kimmel (2006, 2008) points out, men may learn how to accommodate social change and remain masculine within all-male spaces. In these spaces, men play out their versions of manhood without having to defend them. The male space, then, can be both a refuge from and a defense against perceived social change. I learned that barbershopping could be such a space in which conventional men may experience deep emotions consistent with their senses of manhood. Within that space, I discovered a social form that the Christian men I sang with called "manly singing."

Doing Manly Singing

Barbershop singers, and particularly chorus directors, repeatedly refer to barbershop singing as "manly singing," by which they mean a full, rich blend of voices with a dominant bass component, and a particular stress on the ringing chord, which I will discuss later. To understand fully what "manly" means, I will describe the context in which the phrase is typically used.

Truck drivers, carpenters, and brick masons stood at my sides at rehearsals and performances. Bantering, ritualized insults, handshaking, and an occasional mildly off-color word play (not fit to do when wives visit) are common in the weekly rehearsals. For example, when practicing choreography for a song, learning when to "clap" in a song, nearly always elicits some snicker from a chorus member—an allusion to the sexually transmitted disease. Or, a ginger snap cookie becomes a "gender snap" in an elliptical allusion to sexual intercourse. As described by Connell (2005), Connell and Messerschmit (2005), Messner (1993), Ross and Mirowsky (1984), the choruses in which I sang were composed of men with traditional masculine identities.

In their appearances, barbershop singers would never be mistaken for avant-garde musicians: no earrings, flamboyant taboos, or grungy fashion. Rehearsals often start with the singing of the "Old Songs," which depicts a bygone place where even the police say, "How do you do?" Sentimental expressions abound in the lyrics of songs and in the affable greetings extended to visitors and members alike. The music itself has a predominant bass (manly) sound, and men who sing the high tenor parts are often kidded about using their "girlie" voices (a reference to singing in falsetto).

Barbershop singing is a highly stylized form of four-part harmony, sung *a cappella*. While there are several sounds that characterize the style, the "ringing chord" is the most important. The ring in a barbershop chord is an acoustical effect, referred to variously as expanded sound, the angel's voice, the fifth voice, or the overtone. It occurs when the upper harmonics in the individual voice notes, combined with heard voices, reinforce each other, strengthening it so that the ringing overtone stands out separately above the blended sound. The effect is audible only on certain kinds of chords, and only when all voices blend precisely. Hearing the overtone is often taken as sign that a singer has become a "barbershopper."

While the origins of barbershop singing are debatable (Averill 2003; Henry 2001), this style of singing enjoyed its greatest popularity when sheet music was the primary means of distributing popular songs. With the advent of the radio, in the 1930s, older forms of entertainment waned and barbershop singing became a hobby supported by a national organization (The Barbershop Harmony Society). Since the 1980s, membership in the society has declined and barbershop officials have pointed to a variety of reasons such as harried lifestyles, the serious commitment of time the hobby demands (Stebbins 1996), and changing musical tastes.

While declining participation in all sorts of volunteer activities is well documented (Putnam 2000, 2007), the trend has not affected community chorus singing in general (The Chorus Impact Study 2009). Currently, according to the Barbershop Harmony Society headquarters' website, membership is holding steady at about 25,000, and initiatives are underway to attract new members, including major efforts to reach younger singers. I mention declining membership and efforts to recruit new members to underscore the anachronistic nature of the hobby. Anachronisms are intrinsic to the barbershop habitus, and concealed within them is a worldview.

Joe Barbershopper's World View

Joe Barberhopper is the moniker frequently used in Barbershop Harmony Society (BHS) literature to refer to the typical barbershopper. I use it here to depict my fellow barbershoppers. While the BHS strives for a wide appeal, there can be no denying that the typical barbershop singer is middle to old-aged, middle income, a church member, white, and he is decidedly conservative, politically, and socially. Although BHS's code of ethics prohibits political discussions, casual occurrences reveal the conservatism of the hobby. For example, during the 2004 presidential campaign, one chorus member circulated a joke about John Kerry's military service on the listserv for the chorus. The chorus director quickly reminded members about the prohibition against politicking, and the culprit quickly apologized, saying that the posting was an accident of cyberspace.

Still, given the patriotic songs that elicit strong emotions from singers; the backgrounds of the men in business occupations, engineering, construction and independent contracting; and the relatively large numbers of military veterans and church members, I learned to think of my fellow singers as socially conservative. I collected prayers that were given to commence the proceedings at annual installation banquets. One such prayer aptly illustrates my conclusion. In it, we thanked the Lord for living in a country where "the police would not break up a meeting such as ours." I learned to appreciate the "no politics" and "no religion" prohibition, to avoid confrontation with fellow singers over what I saw as a mixture of religiosity and politics in songs such as "God Bless the USA," and in some of the misogynistic and racist lyrics of songs written in the early twentieth century and late nineteenth. For example, "husbands tie their wives up with a ball and chain," (from, "Sentimental Gentleman from Georgia," or "the people are gay," originally "darkies are gay" from "My Old Kentucky Home"). The phrase "darkies are gay," which is Stephen Foster's original lyric, seems to live in the barbershop collective memory. Whenever the song is rehearsed, I would often hear someone in the chorus refer to the original lyric— "you know that used to be 'darkies.'"

No doubt many singers are drawn to fellowship with men who share their conservative predilections, even if the values and points of views they espouse remain, for the most part, tacit. I draw this conclusion from the numbers of singers who belong to the same church, play golf together, and discuss off-limit subjects in these settings.

However, the conservative milieu of barbershopping does not, in it of itself, account for the lure of the hobby. One workshop leader suggested that the emotional reaction to the commonly used harmonic structure in this music, the "ringing chord," is something genetic, implying that a kind of biological tie exists among barbershop singers. "We all hear the 'fifth' voice," he said; "And, we all respond emotionally to it." While not all barbershoppers agree with such biological determinism, most will attest to the thrill that comes from ringing a chord. Emphasis on the ringing chord shapes the selection of songs, and these are mostly songs from the 1920–1940s, though there is a trend to include a few more "contemporary songs" (1960–1980), such as Beatles and Beach Boy selections.

Doing Nostalgia and Sentimentality

Prima facie, the barbershop world is nostalgic, even anachronistic, but for what purposes is the past revered and preserved? Davis (1979) wrote that what most forms of nostalgia seem to have in common is dissatisfaction with the present in service of some end, about which there is consensus. Nostalgic feelings, moods, and social activities, he suggested, range from restoring automobiles to, in extreme cases, reactionary political movements. In the case of barbershoppers, while they share a general malaise about contemporary society, they are particularly dissatisfied with the popular music scene. Barbershop, then, shares this characteristic with other "retro" forms of music, such as bluegrass or old-timey music. Intricate melody, harmony, and lyrics with several verses comprise the core of the barbershop sound, in contrast to popular music, which is often lyrically simple and rhythmically driven. Furthermore, while nostalgic popular song lyrics do exist, most popular music engages the present. Blau demonstrated that popular music is "related to forms of social dislocation and alienation and is largely a reflection of prevailing economic inequalities" (Blau 1988, 883).

One show of which I was a part featured a quartet doing a parody of a rap song. While skillfully performed, audience and chorus members alike seemed relieved when the song was finished, and that number was dropped from the chorus repertory. Rap, and even most popular music, is dissonant with the cognitive and emotional processes that use senses of time for imagining the past in terms of the present (Mead 1932; Flaherty 2001). In other words, the present is too imminent—even as a parody—in the rap form.

Participation in the barbershop hobby creates a space between contemporary society and actually being in that society. Through their music, barbershoppers distinguish between their interpretation of society and their membership in it. They are obviously in society, but they are able to maintain distance from what they see as "negatives" such as popular music, fashion trends, politics, and news headlines, through singing nostalgic songs. One chapter member put it this way:

> I just don't listen to popular music. When I was young, I was a fan of the Beatles, The Eagles, Chicago, even the Kingston Trio and the Beach Boys. I could tell you the titles of songs on the top ten list. Today, I don't even know if there is a "top ten list." Seems like the really popular songs are rap, or hip hop. . . I don't know, I guess I'd be pretty lost in today's music world. Good thing I have my barbershop. I have barbershop CDs in my car and that's pretty much what I listen to. (field notes 2008)

During times of social transition, nostalgia assists people in their understandings of what is happening to their place in a changing social world (Davis 1979). By constructing a version of what the past was like, people can sharpen and define meanings that they want to make important in the present. Like Davis, Wilson (2005), who studied a variety of efforts to resurrect the past, agrees with Davis that nostalgia can help facilitate the continuity of identity. When people perceive threats and obstacles to constructing and maintaining coherent and consistent senses of self, they can shore up their identities through remembering, recalling, reminiscing, and having other emotional experiences associated with doing an imagined past. Individually and collectively, the past is remembered, and, in this act of recall, it is re-created. The lyrics of a barbershop arrangement of the Peter Allen song, "Everything Old Is New Again" (1974) capture this function of nostalgia: "Don't throw the past away, you might need it some rainy day . . . everything old is new again."

Nostalgia may embody contradictions created by technologically-driven social change (Davis 1979). A goal of the international organization is the preservation of a style of music that had its golden age one hundred years ago during vaudeville. That effort has resulted in the world's largest archive of sheet music through the Barbershop Harmony Society, which ironically, is now available online (www.barbershop.org). Practicing one's part at home, assisted by listening to a CD or an electronic file of the song, has become the primary way that new songs are learned in a chorus or quartet. With these technological aids, singers hear their part emphasized—tenor, lead, baritone, or bass—as they sing along.

Much of the old music, including barbershop arrangements of newer music (typically 1950s doo-wop), consists of love songs, songs of love lost, and, most importantly, songs of sentimentality. Some songs, such as "Friends," (composed by Michael W. Smith, contemporary Christian musician and song writer) are religious, and impart meanings to life events, such as the death of a friend or loved one: "But, we'll keep you close as always, it won't even seem you're gone, because our hearts . . . will keep the love strong." Another example, "If the Rest of the World Doesn't Want You," a song from the 1920s (Gerber and Dreyer, Irving Berlin, Inc.), offers reassurance to the prodigal son that home and family are always a safe haven: "If the rest of the world don't want you, then go back to your mother and dad . . . You will always be welcome back home."

Such lyrics, sung with facial expressions embracing both joy and sorrowful empathy are sung by men whose own children are grown, living their lives separate from their parents, or in some cases, by men whose adult children have returned to the "nest." In this context, the lyrics of this song seem incongruent with actual circumstances of everyday life, at best, and tragically poignant, at worst.

Some barbershop singers relate that certain songs carry such strong emotions that they have difficulty singing through them without a cracking voice or even a tear in their eye. For example, my quartet sang "Lean on Me" by Bill Withers to our chorus, and one member related that the song was especially emotional for him, given the help that members of the chorus gave him and his family during his period of unemployment. Or, during my own divorce, rehearsing the barbershop version of "It Is Well with My Soul," written by Horatio Spafford (circa 1873), required constraint to kept tears from falling.

Nostalgic sentiment then reconciles feelings which are in discord into a harmonic form. Men who appreciate emotion but may not have found ways to blend it into everyday life, may discover in music an instrument of emotional expressivity—a sharp contrast with their quotidian existence. Songs about days gone by allow men a safe distance from the subjects of loss, joy, and romantic love. The lack of contemporariness further depersonalizes the feelings in the songs and, hence, becomes a device for controlling emotions through their ritualized expression. One barbershopper put it this way:

> I come to sing with my friends, to a place where I know I am supported and where I can just have fun. I feel a real connection with my brothers in the society. I have depression and anxiety, but not when I'm with the chorus. Singing about feelings makes me feel good. (field notes 2009)

Creating a Manly Space

Barbershop singing creates a space in which men can be sentimental, loving, and even sensitive without violating the ideologies of masculinity. Touching another man can be part of the warm-up routine. For example, as part of a warm-up exercise, directors often have men on the risers turn to massage the neck of a neighboring singer, and then they direct the chorus to turn the other way to reciprocate the massage. Choruses also choreograph their performances, which requires them to move, gesture, and even dance. Barbershoppers also often wear makeup for performances (lipstick, rouge, and eyeliner). In all these activities, remarks intended to reassert masculinity are common. For example, touching might be accompanied by remarks that distance the touching from a "gay" gesture: "Careful there, young man," or "Don't get too used to this." And jokes about wearing makeup for performances are also commonly heard: "My, don't you look nice" [voiced in a sarcastic tone].

Social space conducive to masculine emotional expressivity, minimally, should have characteristics that allow for both expressivity and masculine ideology. Although Oldenburg (1999) referred to physical locations and locales in describing the third place, that is, places between home and work, he does point out that gender mixing has changed the character of previously all-male third places between work and family. These all-male places often served as a refuge within which men could express their emotions to one another. Today, barbershop singers preserve the all-male place by gathering in churches, retirement homes, schools, or virtually anywhere they can rehearse and store risers, wardrobes, and music. These are not third places like a neighborhood bar, but they function as such. For example, while visitors are always welcome at rehearsals, whenever women (wives, daughters, granddaughters, or friends) are present, behavior changes, almost as if one were in a men's locker room and someone yells, "woman in the house!" I have attended coaching sessions with female leaders, and discovered that female directors (allowed by BSH rules), voice, and performance coaches attest to the creed of "manly" singing, just as do male directors. Chorus directors model the way men express emotions through voice and gesture. They demand a full, rich blend of voices with a dominant bass component, and barbershop songs, whether ballads or up-tunes, will include a full (loud) ringing chord here and there in the song. Barbershop songs typical end with ring, achieved by arranging chords into a "tag."

In other contexts, such as choral music, these same musical components might be referred to as rich or full. In the barbershop world, the "manly" designation serves to compensate for the suspicion that singing might be unmanly. Men who are unsure about the way they might be perceived as singers can reassure themselves of their traditional masculinity by thinking of what they do as "manly" singing.

Whatever a director or coach may intend, singers understand manly singing as a kind of folk model of the way men sing. Barbershop singers hear, *post hoc ergo propter hoc*, in their training, a masculine form for the expression of emotions. This habitus is, of course, comprised of directors' and singers' understandings of masculinity, and the ways they impute meanings to their singing. Singers are taught that barbershop singing is emotional, and that emotion must be communicated to audiences. Hence, they must learn to match their facial expressions and body posture with the sentiments of the music they sing, which further creates a situation conducive to sharing feelings, even if it is highly ritualized. The barbershop chorus or quartet becomes, then, a safe haven for the expression of a surprisingly wide range of emotions, especially if a director makes that safe by rewarding expressiveness with praise. Emotions, however, are embedded in the songs, and may or may not be shared conversationally with fellow barbershoppers. The songs become a kind of safe conduit through which emotions may be expressed without identifying ties to an individual singer.

While emotional meanings become specific to place and inclusive of others, they retain an overall theme of masculinity. I have seen men cry, and I have cried, myself, as we sing songs, which elicit "real-world" recollections such as divorce, financial problems, and death of a family member. In this context, "men do cry," and eliciting sufficient emotional content to evoke crying may be expected in the learning a song. Of course, crying must be controlled and suppressed in order to perform a song and carry out a rehearsal or a performance. This is accomplished primarily through part-by-part practice and repetition (cf. Haiman 1998). Too much repetition can, of course, deprive a performance of emotional depth. Therefore, a balance between elicited emotions and control of them is the goal of an accomplished singer. Singing songs about times gone by, for instance, allows men a safe distance from the subjects of loss, joy, and romantic love. The lack of contemporariness depersonalizes the feelings in the songs so that an audience knows that the song is about something or someone else, not the singers themselves.

Making music together, then, creates a fairly predictable, safe form through which men connect in ways that allow them to express emotions prohibited by traditional masculinity (Schutz 1971; Vannini and Waskul 2006). Even the simple choreography that singers learn for concerts can be opportunity for men who "don't dance" to step lively and playfully with other guys.

Serious Leisure and Serious Emotions

Barbershop singing as a hobby can impart meaning to otherwise boring and routine habits of everyday life. Serious leisure time activities (Stebbins 1976, 1982, 2007, 2009) may function as organizational foundations for imparting meaning to ordinary activities. There can be little doubt that barbershopping is serious leisure. It requires a significant commitment of time and finances (practice, membership fees, travel costs, etc.) And, it serves as an organizing principle for daily life, often encroaching on time normally allocated to family and even work.

According to Stebbins (2007), the role that serious leisure plays in modern society approaches institutional portions. Whereas foundational institutions such as family and religion may be less effective in defining and clarifying transformative meanings and anchoring identities, leisure time pursuits may provide and generate complimentary and even novel interpretative processes.

For example, in their description of how men deal with competition in choral singing, Faulkner and Davidson (2006) stress what they refer to as "homo-social" behaviors, that is, specifically masculine ways to compete and cooperate. They write, "Men's perception of singing in harmony implies that this vocal behavior is not only a metaphor for human relationships, but an essential and enriching way of relating to others, fulfilling basic needs for vocal and social connectedness" (Faulkner and Davidson 2006, 219). Barbershoppers, similarly, feel affinity for fellow members, particularly during times of hardship and illness. Their relationships may be like family in some incidents, yet they are rooted in participating in a hobby.

Participation in serious leisure has implications for senses of belonging or community (Stebbins 2007). Leisure time organizations are often seen as a way to escape, or, at least mitigate, negative forces outside of the chorus. In a gender-polarized setting where participation requires constant evaluations of one's own and one's fellow singers' performances, emotions can become raw. I have seen men who have been criticized walk out of a rehearsal. I have been criticized myself to the point of questioning whether my efforts to sing perfectly are worthwhile. Once, when I was asked to stand off the risers, because I had not passed my session leader's audition to assess my mastery of a song, I felt so ashamed that I just left the rehearsal. I seriously considered quitting the chorus, but I decided that I needed to accept being criticized in order to continue learning about barbershopping.

Accepting criticism is not easy for conventionally masculine individuals, and criticism takes on many forms. I have witnessed members criticizing fellow members for their lack of commitment, unreliability, and unwillingness to work toward perfection in singing. These negative characterizations can always find their way back to the singer by way of rumor and innuendo. And, singers rather quickly develop a reputation as a quick learner, a quartet perfectionist, a good guy, but not a particularly good singer and infrequently, "a hard guy to get along with." However, while these factors can be contributing to declining memberships and inactivity, they are only a part of total emotional context of barbershop singing. That context includes deeply instilled senses of membership that transcend evaluations of performance.

For example, a long-time member of a local chorus stands in front of the chorus and relates the story of his fall from a ladder while he was trimming trees at his home. He was hospitalized for several days and suffered considerable pain. He finished his story in this way.

Why am I telling you guys this? Because I want to thank you for calling to see how I'm doing, for visiting me and for me knowing that my buddies are thinking about me. You know I'm 84 years old. Going through this ordeal has made me think more about my death. I have decided I don't want to be displayed and look nothing like myself. I want to be cremated, and I want you guys to sing at my funeral. I want you to sing "Amazing Grace" and the the Lord's Prayer. (my recollection of the story)

There was a short silence after Gene finished his talk. Then, one member retorted, "Hey, Gene, when should we schedule you in?" Laughter filled the rehearsal room, as Gene sat down. Still, we all knew that a solemn commitment had just been made to Gene, a commitment that was kept two years later.

In another example of the emotional ties that singers develop through their interpretations of barbershop songs, Allen, a section leader, explained to the chorus how we could evoke emotions within ourselves to enliven our performance of a particularly sentimental song. "Selling" your song to the audience involves achieving symmetry between the meanings of the lyrics and facial and bodily expressions of the singers. Allen started to talk about his first divorce and, his return to his parents' home for comfort and recovery. His narrative was to prepare us for singing "If the Rest of the World Don't Want You," by thinking of personal experiences in which we were welcomed home after a difficult time. As he spoke, he lost his composure and began to weep. He returned to the risers, while others sat in silence (one member quietly snickered to another that he, himself, has been divorced three times and is quite used to it). Then, the director of the chorus explained how barbershoppers are a close-knit group of men who are accepting of the expression of emotion.

A particularly telling display of barbershop emotional expressivity occurred when a longtime director of my chorus announced he was moving to another town to accept a better job. To us all, he wrote the following email:

> There is no way to convey how much I love you and how much my life and passion for singing have been enhanced by your friendship, encouragement, and joy of singing together over these past 27 years. You are my friends and family. . . . I can tell you as a fact that there is no place on earth, no joy like being in front of you, my friends, as we kid around together, tell stories and jokes (even the bad ones, Frank), sing tags together, learn new things together, and then sing and perform like champions together. . . . (Email from the director, Herman, to chorus members 2011)

A farewell cerebration of his tenure as director was hastily arranged for the last hour of his last rehearsal with us. Chorus members gave testimonies to how Herman had enriched their singing and their lives. While farewell events such as this one are rituals of appreciation, this one simply gushed with effusiveness. Men proclaimed publicly that they loved each other, that they had established bonds of deep emotional connection. "I love you guys," followed by a hug, was the order of the event.

I doubted the sincerity of some of the testimony, as I thought of Goffman's (1959) dramaturgic metaphor, which unpacks such displays as staged role-playing. Knowing that relationships between Herman and members of his quartets had been strained by misunderstandings and broken commitments and that members of the chorus often stifled negative reactions to grueling practices in search of the "perfect" sound, I was aware of a feigned sincerity in what I observed.

Still, within the barbershopper identity, two functions were accomplished during this event: showing appreciation for the director's devotion to and energy expended on the chorus, and doing this in a way fully consistent with a barbershop habitus. Sentimentality framed the narratives of Herman's biography through the frequent use of "love," and references to friendships and ongoing commitments to the barbershop community provided the nostalgia.

As my review of literature showed (Schwalbe 1996, Gallagher and Wood 2005), masculine identities may encompass a considerable range of emotions. They do this by framing the emotions within larger value structures. In the context of the barbershop hobby, effusive praise and feigned sincerity create relationships that are mostly limited to the barbershop world. Just as facial expressions, bodily posturing, and ringing chords enliven sappy lyrics, feigned sincerity and practiced display animate appreciation and praise.

Varieties of Barbershop Identities

Involvement in the barbershop world inevitably results in an individual acquiring a sense of a singer's self. When a singer learns to think about himself as capable of making judgments and generating performances that embody the ways of barbershopping, he acquires a habitus (Bourdieu 1984). For example, as I learned to see differences between qualities of barbershop singing, I acquired a kind of capital that enabled me to judge others and myself according to a practical logic. An official BSH coach explained to one of my choruses that singers can be classified according to their progress toward becoming an ideal barbershop singer. He introduced a model that illustrates the process whereby a singer acquires skills to perform songs without errors and with a high degree of confidence (see Table 1.1). Of course, this model is an idealization, but it captures the distinct judgments, style, and, particularly, the capital of the barbershop habitus.

Table 1.1. Idealized Model of Singer

Aspects	Error-Free Singing	Errors in Singing
Self-Aware	Journeyman	Apprentice
Natural (nonreflexive)	Master	Novice

According to the model, novice singers have a desire to sing but they have acquired neither skills nor the necessary self-awareness. An apprentice has acculturated the style, adopted the values of barbershopping, heard the ringing chord, and even been a part of producing it, but his competency is incomplete. He still sings with errors (wrong notes, rhythms, or words). The journeyman singer gets notes and words correct and even manages the theatricality of singing with emotion, but he does so in a self-conscious fashion, always thinking ahead to the next bar or the next gesture. One director, in admonishing the journeyman-like performance of his chorus, said that he could see singers "reading the words, notes and moves from the back of their eyeballs." Finally, the master singer performs the particulars of a song, error free, without awareness of his agency, that is, non-reflexively. His competency causes his performance to seem natural and effortless.

Of course, this formal way of describing the singer's habitus does not cover the distinctions that individual chorus members make about themselves and others as barbershoppers. The idealized model glosses the informal distinctions, judgments, and categorizations that singers impute to one another. For example, here are some terms that men use to characterize one another as well as them themselves. A "mush mouth" singer sings with a "dead mouth," that is, he fails to articulate or clearly shape his sounds. The resulting sound seems "mushed." A "scooper" tends to find the right note by rising to it, that is, beginning notes to phrases, verses, or choruses of a song are sung initially slight flat. The effect is to scoop the note. A "bottom-sider" sings consistently at the bottom of a note and has to work to "get on top" of the note. Some men have a "harsh" voice, which means that their voices stand out from the chorus or quartet. "Harsh" voices must be muted to blend into a unit sound so that a chord may ring. There are "warblers," or men who have difficulty controlling the vibrato of their voices. Some singers are "clowns," continually cracking jokes, making snide remarks, and, often in return, being the brunt of jokes.

One member, named Ernie, played this role for so long that corny jokes, any retort, any pun, or "bad" joke would be referred to as an "Ernie." For example, whenever the director would critique a performance for lacking emotion, we could expect someone to say, "You mean you want us to sing it with feeling," to which the chorus would collectively respond with, "Ernie."

Barbershop identities are fluid, but sometimes they become, within this small world, fixed. Singers who are "journeymen," may retain that identity for decades, never becoming a master, rarely given an opportunity to sing in a quartet with the best voices in the chorus. "Clowns" may be so for an entire career. "Scoopers" may find that they have a hard time joining a quartet, and "bottom-siders" discover that they are always placed on the riser in front of a mastersinger. As long as these men accept and practice within the identity they have acquired, they remain members with a barbershop habitus.

Within the fraternity, there are several forms of friendship, ranging from intimate to distant, but all are within the context of sentimentality. Members may be known only by their first name on a name tag, but they are greeted warmly at the beginning of rehearsals, chatted with at break-time, and they may even receive a telephone call as a reminder of a performance date or practice time. Such relationships do not penetrate the private lives of the members, but they function as entry to further conversation and deeper relational bonds. Most importantly, they are framed as masculine friendships, shaped by jokes, stories of life events such as illnesses, work stresses, what happened at the office today, and so on. Complaining about life is not expected to elicit any specific kind of response—merely a listening ear. Such is the social capital of barbershopping.

Another aspect of barbershop capital is the deeply ingrained custom of the "after glow." The after glow is an informal get together following a performance, usually an annual show, that takes place at a local restaurant. Members, their spouses, friends, and family eat together, and quartets sing some of their repertoire they did not sing on the show. When these after-the-show events happen, they "take over" the restaurant by unashamedly singing for the entire clientele, whether said group likes it or not.

Some barbershoppers stay engaged in their hobby for decades (one particular barbershopper had been a member of the Society for over sixty years) and barbershop singing often is intergenerational, as in my case. Deep, sincere bonds may develop among those who have sung together for such a long time. During periods of illness, chorus members may visit each other, and the wives of the older members may extend a network of caring that could include food brought to the member's house. These circles of helping friends are common, and resemble the caring networks found in mainstream American churches.

Some singers establish friendships that extend into their private lives. They may socialize, dine at one another's homes, join the same golf clubs, and attend the same churches. However, establishing close friendships is not necessarily a consequence of long-time barbershopping. The bonds they form often symbolize a commitment to the style of singing, and a sense of brotherhood, but not necessarily a compatibility of lifestyles.

More often than not, the deepest bonds form from the practice of quartetting: the formation of quartets from members of a chorus. Managing a quartet over time involves a great deal of emotional work. Singers have senses of their own competencies and voices, and, of course, these sensibilities may be at odds with the judgments of their peers. Some quartets sing together for years and even decades, while others endure for only a few months. Barring uncontrollable events such as a job transfer, job loss, death, or illness of the singer or a member of his family, a quartet has a life span that is dictated by the emotional work that goes on within it.

Usually, a quartet will have a dominant member who has taken the initiative to form the quartet in the first place. In one chorus I sang with, these leaders were referred to as "alpha males." Of course, two alpha males in one quartet can result in struggles for control over when rehearsals are scheduled, where they held, song selections, and vocal and lyrical interpretations. Some quartets are more egalitarian than others, but most adhere to the leader's tastes and sense of order.

Quartets must register with the Barbershop Harmony Society. Their members must be BSH members and pay a nominal registration fee for a unique name, that is, one that is not currently in use. Quartet names are not unlike the names of racehorses. They must be unique, catchy, and, if possible, share some theme with the chorus from which they were formed. For example, Gem Tones formed out of the Diamond State Chorus (from Arkansas, the Diamond State), and MO-Sound from the Sho-Me Statesmen of Missouri (the Show Me state). However, most names are idiosyncratic, as in The Noise, or they may be a play on names, as in Vocal Spectrum, derived from the highly successful chorus, Vocal Majority from Dallas, Texas.

As a part of emotional work, quartets develop means of coping with the hurt feelings of its members. Each decision made about song selection, interpretation of a lyric, or sound production can be a flash point for hurt feelings, conflicts of opinion, and differing tastes. Examples of such means are emails of apology and public apologies in front of the chorus. However, the typical way those feelings are dealt with is by ignoring them, joking about them, or leaving the quartet, claiming with claims of being too busy to continue quartetting.

While there are emotional difficulties and dynamics in quartetting, deep friendships often form that involve quartet members in the details of each other's lives. Wives, family members, and even employers may become involved in a quartet's social life. Airplane flights, automobile trips, time off from work, commitments to singing, as in rehearsal time, gigs, etc., all can create opportunities for friendships that are deep, but distinctively male: that is, they are in the context of accomplishing a task (doing barbershop music) and they are framed mostly by lighthearted banter, jokes at others' expense, and self-deprecating humor.

CONCLUSIONS

Relying on my own experiences and my observations of others, I offer descriptions and analysis that show that within the distinctive context of the barbershop hobby, conventionally masculine men learn to be sentimental and nostalgic. They find in the gendered space that their hobby affords them a way to express emotions that accommodates their conventional understandings of masculinity, while permitting them a range of expressivity not found in their daily lives. By acquiring a habitus, men create avenues for expressing emotions that would otherwise be curtailed as incongruent with conventional masculinity. For barbershoppers, their hobby takes on significance for them because it serves as platform for interpreting their location in society. Through the use of nostalgic lyrics and a theory of harmony, they construct a social world and acquire identities.

For mostly conservative, middle-aged men morphing masculine values into emotionally sensitive performances is no mean accomplishment. This ironic transition is accomplished through several devices that are part of the barbershop habitus: that is, men learn in the barbershop world how to be sentimental and nostalgic, and they use these performances to establish a sense of identity for themselves and their relationships with other barbershoppers. First, the formulaic nature of barbershop singing is conducive to emotional responses. The way dissonances resolve, the way harmonics are constructed for hearing four parts most of the time, the ringing of chords at the ends of phrases, and the addition of "tags" to the body of songs all contribute to the singer's sense of emotionality. The form provides a comfortable distance between the emotions expressed in a song and those felt or lived through emotions of the singer. Second, self-awareness about the emotionality of the songs and performances is achieved through a theatrical framing of the emotions: that is, singers are trained to feign emotions (smiles on faces). This further separates singers from the emotions elicited by the music they sing. Finally, songs about the past create a distance that protects the singer from self-revelation.

Barbershopping affords men opportunities to connect emotionally with each other in ways that are perceived as masculine, even if these perceptions are specific to the hobby and revolve around emotions not typically understood as masculine. The rituals, traditions and customs of the hobby provide the structure within which men may be sentimental and nostalgic, and this, it turns out, is manly singing.

NOTE

1. Parts of this chapter were previously published in *Journal of Contemporary Ethnography*. 2012. Vol. 41: 581–606.

Chapter Two

Wimps Need Not Apply

The Construction of
Masculinity in Youth Wrestling

I am in the NCAA wrestling hall of fame. Well, sort of. Let me tell the story. I was mediocre high school wrestler, an intramural champion wrestler in college, an assist coach for youth wrestling, a faculty sponsor for a wrestling club at Missouri State University. I wrestled in the Show-Me games at age 57 and came in second place. And my son was an outstanding high school wrestler and competed in college for three years until his program was canceled in his senior year. I remain an avid fan and I closely follow the goings on in the wrestling world. Wrestling is personal to me. When I watch a close match, I "feel" every move and I am exhausted as if I had wrestled myself.

But what about this hall of fame claim? My son and I trekked to Oklahoma to visit family when he was a teenager. We visited the hall of fame on the Oklahoma State University campus. This was my first visit, and obviously the first for my son. As we toured the facility, I noticed busts of some legendary wrestlers. One bust was for Terry McCann, the first American wrestler to win an Olympic gold medal at the 1960 games. You could listen to story of Terry's wrestling career on a telephone receiver attached to display. Terry competed for Iowa University and was a national champion. He has a degree in engineering and had a job in Tulsa with oil company. In those days, athletes largely trained on their own for the Olympics. Terry, the story went on the tell, trained at the YMCA in Tulsa. The year was 1960, and I was wrestling for Tulsa Central High School. Because training partners were difficult to find, Tom would ask the entire team to come to the Y after school. As part of his training, he would line us up against the wall in the wrestling room, and gesture to us come out and wrestle with him. While none of us were a match for him, all of us in short bursts of our best moves could give him a good work out. I remember being pummeled by this little man, and the reference to Terry McCann's training in Tulsa is my implied membership in the hall of fame. It's a stretch, I know, but just telling the story gives me a personal connection with the world of wrestling.

What follows is an account of how wrestling becomes an activity in which sports, gender and community intersect to give meaning to masculinity and femininity.

Boys and young men (and increasingly girls and women) dressed in singlets with specially designed shoes ready to wrestle on mats stretched across a high school gym floor. They are present for a wrestling tournament. They range from as young as 6 years old to high school age. They are accompanied by a parent, a father, or even their family including siblings. What they are doing looks all the world like a kind of fighting. It is that, but more it is USA youth wrestling, sponsored competition under the sanction of a national organization. These young people are engaged in an ancient form of competition that teaches techniques to control and subdue one's opponent.

How can an aggressive and brutal form of competition teach a form of thinking about other people that fosters caring and even compassion? Are these young athletes learning the be vicious fighting machines? Is there something about the sport in which they are engaged that contributes to a form of consciousness of the other that expands senses of masculinity and femininity beyond the popular conception of the male athlete as a self-centered, egoist, or worst an insensitive brute, and young women as passive, self-effacing and weak?

Some sociologists claim to have uncovered within the world of sports a what they call "masculine hegemony." For example, as far back as 1989, Messner claimed that Fine's ethnography of boys playing organized baseball ignored the negative effects of learning misogynous attitudes and overly aggressive competitive values. More recently, Messner (2002) laments the lack of television coverage of what he assesses as a social movement of women in sports. He attributes this lag in coverage to a masculine formula employed by television that is actually anti-woman. Messner develops his feminist critique of sports into an analysis of how masculinity, at least in the world of sports, turns out to be anti-feminine (Messner 1990). Along with Montez de Oca (2005), Messner links alcohol consumption by men and exploitation of women with masculine meanings of sports.

In one of the few ethnographically informed reports on wrestling, Curry (1993) deals with how the concepts of body that wrestlers develop can lead to serious injuries and bodily abuse. Finally, a survey study suggests that attitudes of masculinity found in sports can be linked causally to support for the US invasion of Iraq (Stempel 2006).

Masculinity in sports literature, then, seems something just short of a monster. This characterization rests mostly on conclusions drawn from television coverage, advertisements, and recollections of participation in sports. Within cultural anthropology, however, themes of masculinity have been researched ethnographically. Gilmore (1990) argues that certain pan-cultural themes of manhood exist, at least for selected cultures, and that these themes are responses both to the stresses of "male roles" in a given society and to the specifics of life in that particular social context. Manhood, Gilmore argues, is "earned," "precarious" and distinguished from anatomical "maleness" (Gilmore 1990, 11).

Alter (1993) addresses the role wrestling plays in meanings of masculinity, specifically the male body as resistance to the state. He develops an interpretation of the relationship between body and state, pointing out that the Indian wrestler, the pahalwan, has played a significant role in exemplifying Hindu concepts of the whole of body, mind, and state. In contemporary Indian society, wrestlers' training and disciplines constitute an interpretative stance from which to critique the docile body of modernity. While his analysis goes far beyond the question of what is masculinity, it demonstrates that 1) physicality is culturally bound, and 2) that the meanings and consequences of a seemly esoteric and even "minor" sport can carry information that informs us about the complexity of the sense of body in the context of changing social environments.

How participation in sport embodies and perpetuates senses of body and, hence, gendered identities is further acknowledged in cultural analyses of sumo wrestling. So closely linked are the meanings of being Japanese to the rituals of sumo wrestling that some authors equate a Japanese sense of manhood with being a sumo wrestler (Opler 1945, West 1997). Shinto religion, ritualized violence and feudal society are preserved within the context of contemporary Japanese society in the complex practice of Sumo. While the sumo wrestler's life is communal (West 1997), supported by elaborate and even deviant practices (Duggan and Levitt 2002); still, scholars do not hesitate to take sumo as a cultural exemplar of masculinity. India, Japan, Turkey, Iran, and East African tribes are cultures in which wrestling plays a dominant role in defining identities, both collective and gendered. Certainly, these societies are patriarchal and undergoing rapid and even chaotic change, but the understanding of their core cultural values is furthered from thick descriptions of a male dominated sport, wrestling.

In contemporary Western society, ideals about what a man really is are open to various interpretations and criticisms (Cooky and Messner 2018, Franklin 1989, Messner 1989, 1990, Messner and Sabo 1990, Rotundo 1993). While masculinity is learned "through participation in society," in contemporary society there are many ways to participate, and the requirements of participation in one segment of society may be quite different from those in another.

So, how are we to know a "manly" cultural practice (cf. Gilmore 1990) and are the cultural tenets of manliness transferable to girls and women?

Amateur wrestling in America enjoys nothing like the cultural centrality of Sumo in Japan, or even the status of the pahalwan in India. Still, according to the National Federation of State High School Associations nearly a quarter of a million boys, and about twenty-one thousand girls participate in wrestling. Before the establishment of girl's programs, girls participated in high school wrestling at the lower weights and sometimes with success. These girls were often sisters of older brothers who wrestle. Girls' and women's wrestling has grown, and this growth has played a role in efforts to promote the sport against pressures to eliminate it (see the *New York Times* article, NYtimes. com/March 20, 2007). Women's wrestling has been an Olympic sport since 2004. And, while men's and women's wrestling were to be dropped from the 2020 Tokyo games, both were restated after an international outcry.

Today 26 USA states have wrestling programs for girls, and the NCAA has listed women's wrestling as an emerging sport, which when 40 member institutions have programs will become a sanctioned sport with its own national championship tournament. This growth has occurred while universities and college continue to drop the men's wrestling. Since the 1970s, close to 200 programs have been cancelled, mostly because of the pressures to adhered to the mandates of Title IX, that is, to establish parity between men and women's sports programs. I will return to a discussion of this topic after I describe the culture of wrestling and address the question of whether women's wrestling is distinctive or a feminized form of the wrestling culture.

Recent studies of girls participating in other contact sports, for example, hockey (Theberge 2003) point to feminization process. Still, USA Wrestling (sponsors of youth sports programs nationally) reports a steady growth in participation in wrestling as they sponsor teams, tournaments, and international competitions. Overall, while complicated and difficult to accurately assess, wrestling remains a male-dominated and widely practiced sport in American society.

I sought to uncover the cultural meanings of participation in the world of wrestling, expecting that such meanings might yield a further understanding of at least an aspect of masculinity in American culture. While "contact sports" (boxing, football, and wrestling) are often seen, usually quite negatively, as exemplars of masculinity, only a few researchers have done thorough ethnographic descriptions of what transpires in these sports (Wacquant 1992, 2004). Wacquant's (2004) work is an exemplary exception. He uncovered a supportive, tight-knit web of norms, rules, and social action that connected with the realities of life in South Chicago. In this study, the social life of the boxing gym is inseparable from social conditions of inner-city life for African-Americans. Yet, the world of boxing, through Wacquant's accounts of his participation in it, emerges as tough and violent, but ritualized and controlled. The image of desensitized brutes pummeling each other into early dementia gives way to a portrait of men creating a special reality that reflects both their struggles and the valor of their adaptations to social forces beyond their immediate control.

Believing that the types of activities in which young males participate may provide opportunities for learning about gendered social action, I conducted an ethnography of amateur wrestling. My intent was to discover a strong version of the meaning of masculinity among young men between the ages of eight and eighteen. I examined the organization of the world of amateur wrestling and the support roles played by fathers, mothers, and other family members. I attended wrestling tournaments over a six-year period; worked out with high school wrestlers; assisted with coaching at a youth wrestling club; joined wrestling organizations to receive their newsletters and other publications; and interviewed parents, coaches, and wrestlers. I also helped established a wrestling club at a university and competed, myself, in a statewide tournament.

What I discovered was that youth wrestling, like most voluntary youth sports (cf. Nash and Lerner 1981), is built on beliefs about the importance of competition within a context that resembles the organization of family life. A parent is usually involved, or in the case of clubs from inner cities, a coach may assume fatherly roles, providing rides to practices, meets, and often serving as an emotional mentor and even disciplinarian. In this sense, the context for socialization may be seen as institutional, or as Irvine (1999) has described this phenomenon, as institution-lite. When young men participate in wrestling, they learn developmental and moral models for being a wrestler.

THE WORLD OF WRESTLING

Typically, wrestling in American society is organized around a youth program that often maintains loose, unofficial ties to a local high school. Coaches are active in or supportive of such programs; and parents, most often fathers, often former wrestlers themselves, are instrumental in the organization and maintenance of the programs. But each of several programs observed for this work were supported not just by fathers' attitudes toward the sport and their active participation as coaches or assistants, but also by grandparents, mothers, brothers, sisters, and friends of the wrestler's family.

Youth programs in wrestling organize the tournaments by grouping the youth by age and weight: "kids" (ages 8 and under through 14); cadets (ages

14 through 16); and juniors (ages 16 to 18). The season begins in February and continues for the winners into the national tournaments held in June and July. The season consists of practices once or twice a week, usually held at local high schools or community gymnasiums. Dedicated wrestlers in large cities may practice virtually every night, traveling to open practices held by local wrestling clubs at various sites. Then on Saturdays, tournaments are held, usually at local high schools. These tournaments are immense organizational undertakings, since over 700 wrestlers may participate, each requiring weighing, classification by age and weight, and pairing into brackets for competition. Each match must be timed, recorded, and refereed. Volunteers often "man" the tables, while official referees certified through training sessions sanctioned by the USA Wrestling oversee the matches.

On a Saturday, a community high school gymnasium may have as many as fifteen mats stretched out on its floor, with tables by each mat for the timer and scorekeeper. Wrestlers, coaches, and some parents mill around on the floor of the gymnasium, waiting for the match, supporting their teammates, studying their opponents, or simply listening to music through headphones. Other parents and friends fill the bleachers, reading newspapers and waiting for the posting of the brackets. After the matches begin, the noise of whistles, yells, and groans creates a din in which the emotions of victory and defeat hinge on seconds on the timers' clocks. While ten matches are going, idle wrestlers waiting their turns may sleep or rest on the bleachers. The overall effect is to create a buzz of struggles that one can block out while concentrating on the match at hand, or anticipating a coming one. The wrestler must learn to be alert to the complexities of the activities around him, attending to teammates who are competing, knowing when his next match is, and getting himself ready to wrestle.

Although the number of matches occurring may vary from one to twenty or more, each tournament exhibits the same structure. This structure reflects the requirements of accounting for various elements—the matches and their outcomes, the nature of wrestling itself as a "combat sport," and the organizational efforts to establish parity of competition.

The Values of Wrestling

Three varieties of adults transmit the values of the world of amateur wrestling to new young wrestlers: elite wrestlers, coaches, and family members. Elite wrestlers have reputations established primarily in collegiate or international competition. Coaches are often ex-wrestlers, perhaps once of elite status, who devote themselves to running wrestling clubs and to the instruction of young wrestlers. Families of wrestlers are often made up of fathers or other males

who, themselves, were once involved in wrestling, or mothers and other fe-
males who were wrestling cheerleaders or members of families of wrestlers.

These adults of the wrestling world are responsible for the organization and
pecuniary support of the sport. They back local high school programs, belong
to booster clubs for university-level competition, and support local youth
clubs. Their presence is keenly important to the socialization of a wrestler's
identity. They console wrestlers who have lost matches or been injured, and
they set the tone for sportsmanship on and off the mat. Generally, adults
champion hard work, competitive attitudes, and rough, yet rule-governed action, on the mat. An elite wrestler speaking to boys at a summer clinic told
the following story:

> When I was in college, I was having trouble with my grades until I decided to
> put the same kind of dedication and hard work into my studies that I put into my
> wrestling. I graduated with honors, and I achieved most of my wrestling goals. I
> can't say that wrestling was fun. It was work, but it taught me the value of hard,
> goal-directed work. (field notes, 2000)

To wrestle, a young athlete must learn to identify as or "be" a wrestler.
Here I refer to a socialization and training process in which a young man
internalizes notions of the wrestler's body and the moves and strategies of
competitive wrestling, develops a procedure for interpreting the meanings
of competition, and acquires a situation-bound sense of permissible violence
that links him reciprocally with fellow wrestlers. As I will show in the section on Moves, violence or at least aggressive play is framed in wrestling
by permissible moves, rules, but most of all, by the acquisition of a sense of
wrestling grounded in the body and a sense of self in a social context.

Body: In wrestling, as in other sports, a particular body type and performance is valued. Wrestlers are supposed to be strong, agile, and able to
endure great strain. They become elitist about their sport, believing wrestlers
are the toughest, best-conditioned athletes of all sports. For them, participation in wrestling challenges them to shape their bodies through dieting and
weight lifting so that they may achieve maximal performance. Even for high
school wrestlers at the heavier weights, this usually means body fat rates of
4 to 8 percent.

In the weight room, wrestlers follow their own personal training routines.
They tend to invent exercises with weights that emulate wrestling moves,
and they often train with high repetitions. Specifically, a wrestler may do
one hundred repetitions with a light weight on a bench press exercise where
a football player would train with heavy weights and fewer repetitions.
Wrestlers strive for maximum strength within a minimum of mass. Training
routines, therefore, can be highly individualistic.

Not all wrestlers will strive for muscle bulk. Instead, some might refer to a world-renowned wrestler like John Smith (now the Oklahoma State University coach) who relies on agility and strategy to defeat much stronger opponents. In Smith, wrestlers, their coaches, and families find examples of the merging of strategies, moves, and quickness into a style of wrestling not all wrestlers can emulate, but which becomes part of what "body" means in wrestling. Since body attributes in wrestling vary and are contextually sensitive to performance, young wrestlers learn multi-dimensional ways to think of the physical attributes of body. Big boys wrestle a different style from the "water bug" scampering of the lighter boys.

Moves: Learning the moves of wrestling requires an understanding of leverage as it relates to balance and strength. The physics of wrestling must be grasped intuitively by the young wrestler. He must sense when he has the angle on his opponent and when strength can compensate for the lack of leverage. Some of the great teachers of the sport (legends like Oklahoma A&M's legendary coach Ed Gallagher and more contemporary coaches like Dan Gable, John Smith, and Kyle Sanders) have devised drills which teach wrestlers a muscle memory for movement. For example, one drill consists of stringing a rope across the wrestling room and having wrestlers "sweep" under it to pick-up an object from the floor on the other side. Widely used terms or wrestling moves are "sweep," "crank," "handle," "drag," "bar," "pin," "tilt," "hook," "pivot," "base," and "post." These are metaphorical in that they remind wrestlers of the mechanical character of their sport. Thus, one's opponent is not objectified in the sport, he is, rather, "mechanicalized." In other words, one's opponent is a set of possible angles, a matrix of body parts coordinated in a movement that generates openings, blocks, and counter-moves. This is a highly complex process often captured in metaphors of levers and pulleys, angles and degrees, and above all else it is understood through reference to elite wrestlers who embody a particular style or variety of body type.

Competition: Even though physiological differences exist among wrestlers within age and weight pairings, each wrestler is supposed to learn the values and skills of the sport so he can utilize his strengths and body type to develop moves that result in successful competition. It is true that some wrestlers dominate their competition, but when wrestling occurs in its ideal form, outcomes are reflections of the internalization of the wrestling values and not just of strength or the mastery of the techniques of the sport. To win is really not enough: in post-match analysis, coaches explain how a match was "ugly" or "beautiful." Ugly ones are those in which moves are poorly executed, or in which a wrestler, even though he wins, fails to set up moves or misses angles, generally giving the impression he lacks skills. Beautiful matches are not necessarily high scoring, but they demonstrate the mastery of wrestling skills. At a Saturday tournament, one can hear cheers of approval for a well-executed move, and in freestyle, where the "throw" exemplifies the ultimate control of one's opponent, spectators are often awestruck by a "high amplitude" throw. Even young wrestlers learn to pride themselves on how they can make a match "beautiful."

Since the nature of the sport involves the exertion of physical energy and violent contact between wrestlers, learning to control one's emotions is important to becoming a wrestler. But the values of being a wrestler involve more than control of emotions; they entail framing them in specific forms. For example, at the finish of a match, coaches and family members or other supporters may offer criticisms of wrestlers' performances. This includes further coaching and the suggestion for more workouts, much like a golfer is advised to work on his weaknesses on the practice tee. Even in victory, the wrestler knows the sport requires constant polishing and drill. He must be receptive to instruction. In fact, this willingness to be coached is a measure of the internalization of the values of wrestling. A young wrestler's receptiveness to coaching is embedded in his attitudes toward violence and sportsmanship.

Coaches, family members, and elite wrestlers approve of some limited expressions of emotions before, during, and after a match. These expressions are pats on the opponent's back, handshakes, the jiggle (a jumping movement used for both the warm-ups before a match and the relief of tension), and very brief celebrations after a victory, consisting of raised arms or jumping. This celebration, always in acceptable forms, lasts no more than a few seconds, and is terminated by the ritual of the referee's raising the victor's hand and the opponents' joining hands in a shake. Some novice wrestlers embarrass themselves in the wrestling world by introducing high-fives and other more theatrical antics they see on televised professional sports. In the world of wrestling, emotion is supposed to be expressed in the context of ritual, with every match being conducted according the same protocol, within the same form that defines the violence of competition according to the limits of fairness and safety. The arbitrator of these rituals is the referee, who infers the intentions and motives of wrestlers and awards points according a complex set of scoring rules, which include disincentives for passivity, brutality, and uncontrolled movements. In a sense, the complex set of judgments that are made by the referees and the wrestler's reaction to these judgments has the effect of framing violence.

Violence: In wrestling, the ritualization of competition functions to frame the expression of violence. Brutality to cause unnecessary pain is forbidden. Of course, this whole matter is clearly "in the eye of the beholder."

The acquisition of the "eye," that is, the interpretative procedures for seeing wrestling, not as brutal, but as sportsman-like competition is a central feature of socialization into the wrestler's world. Consider the following set of rules distributed among members of a freestyle-wrestling club:

It is against the rules to intentionally inflict pain on the opponent by using brutal holds or moves. The wrestler who uses these brutal holds and moves will be disqualified from the tournament. (The head official and tournament director will make the decision for disqualification.) The following situations are considered brutality, as delineated by the Freestyle Rules of the Minnesota Wrestling USA in 2000:

Thrusting knee into opponent's stomach
Fisticuffs
Intentionally fracturing opponent's bones
Intentionally dislocating opponent's joints.
A twisting action to cause suffering.
Driving toward opponent's head when opponent is bridging.
Lifting opponent, who is bridging, and throwing him back to the mat.
(One can only force opponent to the mat without a lift).

Pile driver. If opponent is upside down, wrestler must take his opponent to his side. (Some part of the wrestler's body, other than his feet, must touch the mat before the upper part of his opponent's body touches the mat). This is a potentially dangerous situation, so mat officials stop it when it develops.
Slamming opponent to the mat. If a wrestler lifts his opponent from the mat, he is responsible for his safe return to the mat.
Any illegal hold with intent to injure opponent.

The list of rules codified clearly the forbidden unmanly acts such as pulling hair or ears, biting, pinching, twisting, kicking, head butting, strangling, grasping an opponent's singlet, stepping on the toes of one's opponent, jerking motions, and talking to one's opponent during the match.

These rules turn a violent-looking activity into a "manly form" of competition. Thus, the violence of wrestling is framed within the rules which define "manly" action. For example, it is illegal to use a "hard cross face" (a defensive move in which one wrestler crosses the face of his opponent with his forearm, and then, by applying pressure to the face, forcing his opponent to move). A judgment about just when a "cross face" is "hard" is set within the context of competition. In fact, coaches can be heard to yell at their wrestlers, "Hard cross face!" but they mean that the cross face be applied firmly, not struck as a blow. Wrestlers who allow too much space between their arm and their opponent's face may be cautioned or even penalized for a hard cross face. Wrestlers who apply a cross face with such permissible force that they break the hold their opponent has on them are rewarded either by scoring points or by hearing the joyful exclamations of their coaches, fellow wrestlers, or family members.

The framing of violence as acceptable in certain forms represents the transformation of brutality into manly competitive aggression. The real danger of this sport is thereby minimized through the internalization of the norms of fair competition, respect for the safety of one's opponent, and the proper mastery of wrestling moves. This transformation of brutality into acceptable manly competition is often problematic, and coaches and officials may have to redefine the norms in the course of a season. Hence, referees may change their style and interpretation of the rules in response to an injury. For example, once at a national qualifying tournament for juniors, a young man was thrown and consequently suffered a fractured vertebra in his neck. The throw was cleanly executed and legal, but consensus among the coaches and referees was that the level of violence at that particular meet was a problem, manifesting itself in this one injury. After a meeting of USA Wrestling officials, the word was spread by phone, word of mouth, and through a special pre-tournament clinic, that throws were going to be more closely watched. In subsequent competitions that season, referees were very quick to intervene whenever a wrestler lifted his opponent from the mat, and in close supervision of "potentially dangerous moves."

Toughness: Developing toughness in wrestling is very much like socialization in American culture to be a man. Toughness refers to several dimensions of performance. A tough wrestler endures pain, that is, though he may cry out when injured, he is expected to control his emotions, even if seriously injured. For example, he should not cry or exaggerate the gravity of his injury through writhing on the mat, screaming, and the like. He learns to experience pain silently as a normal part of competition, emitting no more than a grimace, a groan, or a short, low yell when struggling to avoid a fall. When he has a minor injury such as a nosebleed, he continues to wrestle until stopped by coaches or referees, at which point a two-minute injury time-out occurs.

If he cannot return to the mat after the time-out, he forfeits the match.

The tough wrestler struggles with all his might and skill to avoid being pinned to the mat. In fact, value is placed on how hard a young man will fight to avoid being pinned, and this value is independent of winning or losing. Therefore, a wrestler may find a measure of satisfaction from limiting the number times he is pinned in a season. Even if he feels completely mortified upon being pinned, he will later display his toughness by coming out for the next match with an enthusiastic attitude.

In a sense, toughness is what wrestling is all about. It is central among a set of values embodied in the advertising slogan, "Wimps need not apply." A wimp in this context is a wrestler without toughness, a young man not willing to endure training, pain, and the emotion of embarrassment in defeat. Another derogatory term which applies to a type of wrestler is "fish," and while a wimp is not a wrestler, a fish may be. A fish is simply a weak wrestler who flops over during competition. A fish may try to be tough but lacks the necessary physical strength to compete. In wrestling lore, there is hope for a fish, but none for a wimp. Hence, the sport defines not being discouraged or being wimpy as manly. Indeed, as indicated above, since discipline in practice and competition is highly valued, the art of motivation is important in the world of wrestling.

Generally, the values of wrestling are easily discernible. Slogans of various types may be found in wrestling rooms, on tee shirts and even in programs for the matches. Examples of some these are "Six minutes, no excuses, no regrets," "Wimps need not apply," "True grit used here." Slogans function to provide the context for motivation to train, and more importantly for the acquisition of the wrestler's self.

A tough wrestler is one with staying power, a wrestler who gives and takes punishment. He is clean, that is, he wrestles within the limits of the rules. Still, the sportsmanship of being considerate of one's opponent either in defeat or in victory is part of the value nexus of wrestling. At the end of a match, the experience of two wrestlers exchanging words of praise and encouragement, shaking hands, and briefly embracing in sheer exhaustion, one the victor and other the loser, is highly valued. A well-fought or a "beautiful" match rewards both winner and loser by reaffirming the value of toughness that is symbolized in the ceremony of congratulations.

Wrestlers are winners or losers by reputation. This is reflected in the fact that while every wrestler strives to win, not all can accumulate winning records. Those who continue to participate despite losing do so in the hope that in the future they, too, will be winners. However, even those who continually lose develop a feeling of accomplishment in their sense of improvement, which may assume the form of mastering the moves and/or the language of wrestling. For example, in wrestling lore, one gets better through "taking lumps." This means that one wrestles better opponents for the purpose of getting tough and gaining mat-experience. There is no substitute for "taking lumps."

Winning: Of course, the ultimate recognition in any sport comes from winning, from rising to the top of one's competitive division, and there can be little doubt that winning is definitive measure of a wrestler's acumen. To win, one must have internalized the values of the sport, besides acquiring an individual style. A successful wrestler knows how to judge his competition, change his style to counter that of his opponent, and display the values of sportsmanship and team membership. But winning may be understood more broadly than as just a total of points for a match. Slogans on wrestling room walls read, "If you did your best, you won," "The difference between good and great is a little great effort," "Luck is what happens when preparation meets opportunity," or just, "Conceive, believe, and achieve."

While these admonitions may not function as cultural maxims, they are nevertheless more than shibboleths. Coaches, fathers, elite wrestlers, and even mothers use them to help their wrestlers understand what happened to them during competition. A bad call by a referee might result in losing a match by a single point. For example, a high school wrestler fails to receive two back points during a move and loses his match with a score of five to six. He feels wronged and is upset. He sits disconsolate in the corner of the gym. A few teammates walk over to pat him on the back and offer a few words. The coach does his work. He reminds his young wrestler that he did his best and that he knows the true outcome of the match. A few days later, the wrestler remarks that he learned from the match; and the loss will help at the state tournament by serving as a reminder to be more aggressive at the end of a contest.

What I want to demonstrate here is that the question of winning and losing is understood within an interpretive scheme which allows varied meanings of winning, and it compares the effort, honesty, and improvement of wrestlers to a standard of winning. This standard contains moral and literal elements. To be sure, the qualification of winning is literal, but the experience of it is moral and interpretive.

Wrestling is, of course, an individual sport, but is it is also a team sport when high schools and colleges compete in dual meets, or when teams accumulate points at tournaments, or even when clubs compete in freestyle team matches. Hence, wrestlers must learn to think of their training in terms of team membership. As one slogan found on a wall in a wrestling room states:

Losers assemble in little groups to share their misery and to bitch about coaches and guys in other little groups. Winners assemble as a team.

The team is the context for these interpretations of winning, losing, improving, and becoming a wrestler. Again, the parity model interpenetrates the hierarchical form of the sport. To understand outcomes of competition and practice in terms of this hierarchy alone is to miss the dynamics of interaction among team members. "Wrestlers are tight," the saying goes. This means they share a way of seeing what they do, and because they believe others rarely can understand, they develop strong cognitive and emotional bonds among themselves. There is, therefore, a wrestler's solidarity.

Wrestler's Solidarity

Wrestler's solidarity is often promoted and enhanced through reminders of the minority status of the sport and that this is so despite its toughness. Hence, one often sees young and old folks, alike, wearing tee shirts at wrestling tournaments that express contempt for a sport that rivals wrestling. Perhaps the best example of these is a slogan on a tee shirt sold to promote a local wrestling club. It read:

> *The sight I adore on a basketball floor is wrestling mats spread from door to door.*

There are also constant reminders to wrestlers of their status as it is assessed by fellow students and athletes of other sports. In locker room repartee, for example, wrestlers might be accused by peers of being gay, or they are derided for participating in a sport that requires them to come into close contact with each other while wearing revealing uniforms. During these locker room sessions, arguments can be overheard among athletes about the relative skills required by their respective sports. Wrestling, the claim is often made, is just two guys trying to out-muscle each other, or wrestling is an embarrassment to "real" sports, because it is just a show, like professional wrestling. Professional wrestling and its clientele are further portrayed by fellow students as unsophisticated, foolish and for the "uneducated."

Derision of wrestling is commonplace, but it goes beyond the usual ribbing athletes give one another. Linking wrestling to two stigmatized statuses, male homosexuality and exhibitionistic professional wrestling, highlights the context in which wrestling is understood. Of course, wrestlers develop comebacks ("You swimmers are all soft!"; "Yeah, what about you wimpy tennis players?"; and "Why don't you try wrestling sometime?"). Of course, all these defenses address the negative characterization of wrestling as a sport of tough guys with little sophistication, or of masochistic individuals who endure difficult training routines and starve themselves to achieve certain weights.

The overall consequence of these attacks on wrestling is to reinforce in the wrestler's mind the minority status of his sport; and, hence, to strengthen the norms of wrestling and his sense of belonging to the wrestling fraternity. That this association is a fraternity is underscored by the very organization of the sport. A heavy emphasis on the "ideal body" results in distinctive attitudes toward and mannerisms regarding the body. A young wrestler weighs in before competition, and the sight of naked male bodies is common. A typical weigh-in room at a freestyle tournament is full of boys and young men in their underwear. Little effort is made to preserve modesty within the room, or to shield the room from outsiders. Doors are left open, and anyone can walk into the weigh-in room. Women at tournaments learn to preserve boys' modesty by avoiding the open doors or displaying a similar casual attitude toward the sight of boys in their underwear.

The wrestler's immodest attitude toward his body is, of course, situational. The same young boy who switches his singlet from blue to red at mat-side by first stripping to his underwear (red or blue reversible nylon singlets, identify wrestlers for scoring purposes) may be quite shy at the doctor's office or in front of his older sister at home. During a tournament however, the male body is framed as part of the competition, that is, the wrestler's head, arms, leg, and torso are the sport's equipment. Just as the development of equipment is a part of other sports, body development is a part of wrestling. This framing is literal and public. After weigh-in each wrestler's hand is marked with his age and weight category (for example, "Cadet, 156" or "Jr, 178"). For the rest of the day's competition this mark, and the other features of the wrestler's appearance serve to frame his body, according to the organization of the sport.

The Wrestler's Self

A wrestler learns to think of himself as a kind of wrestler; and though he may or may not be thought of by others in this sense, he believes he is. There are two basic kinds of wrestlers—strength wrestlers and finesse wrestlers—and there are several subtypes of each. Essentially a strength wrestler is one who relies on overpowering his opponent basically with brute muscle power. In the youth ranks, these wrestlers are boys who have matured early and possess natural strength; among older and more skilled wrestlers they are young men who have dedicated themselves to intensive weight-training programs. Finesse wrestlers, on the other hand, are known as students of the sport. They are often clever, quick, and skillful in their mastery of the moves of wrestling. To a degree, of course, all wrestlers must be strong, but finesse is often more highly valued. Wrestling with finesse represents the purest type of wrestling for it embodies the ideals of the sport: blending skill, knowledge, and power to control one's opponent.

The finesse wrestler controls his emotions with a comportment that communicates his skill. He is cool, approaching each match with a sense of study. He sizes up his opponent before the match or during the first few seconds of competition. He knows how to defend against a more powerful and aggressive wrestler and can turn the strength of such an opponent to his advantage. He accomplishes this through the manipulation of angles and momentum, taking advantage of his opponent's wild thrusts forward, or that other's tendency to plant himself on the mat to exert his strength. The finesse wrestler will spin around the thrusting, stronger opponent, using his speed and lever-age to score points by gaining control.

Of course, this contrast between skill and strength is essential to virtually all sports, but in wrestling, recognizing these values is essential to an appreci-ation of the competition. Certainly, coaches stress strength or skill in varying proportions, according to what constitutes their image of an ideal wrestler. In all the images of the ideal wrestler, however, both finesse and strength are present and these values merge in an overarching value of toughness among participants in the sport.

The act of wrestling, then, is a dynamic process of continually accumulat-ing knowledge through which a wrestler learns and relearns the basics of his sport. The phrase, "It gets in your blood," describes the attitude of longtime supporters of the sport, as well as of young participants. The idea behind this expression is that once a person learns the values of wrestling, endures the training, and feels victory or defeat, he will always be a wrestler—a person who appropriately displays the emotions associated with wrestling, has inter-nalized its values, and who is habituated to the sport. Indeed, there are many such people. High school wrestlers return to their old gyms after graduation to wrestle with the team. Fathers compete in old-timers' tournaments. A family "adopts" a favorite wrestler to follow and support after their own children's careers are finished, or when young men count the months in anticipation of the start of freestyle season.

Participants and supporters of wrestling can be emotionally connected to the sport with a bond that has little to do with the promise of any reward for the wrestler, such as a scholarship or professional career. Instead, it has to do with the internalization of values. For the wrestler, internalization includes learning the style of wrestling, including the wrestler's walk and the wres-tler's look. The wrestler's walk is a kind of strut, toes forced straight ahead in a deliberate gait with little shoulder movement. The wrestler's look all too often is the result of years of competition that shows in the nose and ears. Noses may be slightly flattened and ears cauliflowered. The cauliflowered, or wrestler's, ear is scar tissue that forms from injuries which cause fluid ac-cumulation in the unprotected ear.

Young wrestlers often see the wrestler's ear as a mark of toughness, an out-ward display of experience on the mat. High school and college rules require the use of protective head-gear, but wrestlers may sometimes practice without protection, and in freestyle head gear is optional. It shows that the wrestler has endured pain and is willing to carry a mark, even a stigma, of the sport. Indeed, the wrestler's ear is considered ugly and a deformity by the general population. But by taking on this physical mark of participation in the sport, wrestlers are validated among themselves and they obtain a distinctive status in the world of sports. Although adults involved in wrestling discourage young wrestlers from thinking this way, and often admonish them when they practice without protection, these same adults may sport the ear themselves, and as their wrestlers gain experience in the sport, they are allowed to decide for themselves whether to risk a cauliflower ear.

In brief, a seasoned wrestler looks the part, his face and body carrying the meanings of his sport with his casual dress reflecting the same. Blue jeans, tee-shirt, baseball cap, and sports jacket are the standard wardrobe. Tee-shirts often announce participation in prestigious tournaments, identify high school or college teams, or display logos of summer wrestling camps.

While a thorough examination of the consequences of acquiring the wrestler's self within the context of solidarity brought on by the minority status and the peculiar juxtaposition of felt superiority and oppression is beyond the scope of this chapter, I have sketched what I think is the dynamic process of constructing a wrestler's world within which the self emerges.

How the Distaff Reconfigures the Form

As women take up activities that were once exclusively male, they not only master and enact the features of the form, they modify it in ways that are consistent with cultural meanings of being female. For example, my wife and I have written about how women singers of barbershop harmony (the Sweet Adelines) feminize the male form of singing. They do this by adding to and modifying the central features of the form. They select gender appropriate songs, they stress a feminine appearance, use more emotive singing and choreography (Nash and Nash 2016).

While barbershop singing and wrestling are divergent activities, both are grounded in an idealized form which I have described for wrestling and we depicted for barbershop singing. How do girl and women wrestlers feminize the world of wrestling? Using internet sources, which are considerable, I suggest that distaff wrestlers embrace all the elements of the wrestlers' self. They cite competition and toughness which they say increases their self-confidence and generalizes motivating them to excel in everyday life. Among the ways that the form is feminized is an emphasis on technique (moves) over strength. This difference was mentioned in the context of competition with men which was the only avenue for participation until the establishment of separate programs. Girls who won against boys in the lower weights did so by mastering the moves. This feature persists and distinguishes the feminized form.

Also, distinct, and hence feminized is the emphasis for how wrestling provides opportunities of women of various body types to participate. What I have referred to as the idealized body type which manifest itself elite men's wrestling as small to large versions of same compacted, low body fat profile.

Among women wrestlers, various types of bodies are found within weight classes and especially in the upper weight classes.

> Wrestling is one of the few sports where you use your body type as a way to get the advantage over your opponent. Tall wrestle short, skinny wrestle stocky. As long as they are the same weight, you must learn how to wrestle whatever your opponent looks like. (Shai 2017)

Fred Davis (1992) in his study of fashion, noted that as women dress "more like men" (pants, business suits, etc.) they employ subtle markers of femininity such as a head scarf or hair clip or a color swatch against a stark masculine backdrop. Female wrestlers in the amateur world similarly feminize their appearance. Although the uniform that both male and female wrestlers wear, the singlet, affords little opportunity for fashion statements, the noticeable and distinctive marker of femininity is hair. While an occasional male wrestler will have long hair, perhaps an Afrio style of long straight hair, the girls and women have carefully braided hair or longer hair to shoulders.

CONCLUSION: BOYS INTO MEN AND GIRLS INTO WHAT?

Amateur wrestling takes place in a domain of thought and action, a world of personal and social meanings, through which many young people come to understand themselves as athletes and as men and women. As is the case with most such activities, wrestling is a world not just of its youthful participants, but also of coaches, parents, and other adults who bear and transmit its culture. While the casts of characters differ from and reflects the surrounding social circumstances of the participation in the sport, the organization of wrestling bears similarities to Wacquant's boxing gym. There are rules to frame violence, conceptions of body, skills of movement, and, above all else, disciplined social action within a normative social context. Resultant senses of the wrestler's self, while no guarantee of a well-integrated existence within an androgynous society, show that blunt descriptions of meanings of masculinity embodied in sport are incomplete and inadequate. Approaches to masculinity in sport that ignore or minimize the lived-through experiences of participation (cf. Messner 2002) while stressing broader connections to individual behaviors such as aggression and self-destruction might foster an unsubstantiated link between masculine hegemony and pathologies of the self. As Wacquant has aptly demonstrated, being a man and a boxer is far more complex than being a brute man. Likewise, uncovering the meanings and consequences of wrestling for young men might show that being a wrestler and being subject to masculine hegemony is problematic. Likewise, while not as well understood, participation in the wrestling world does not seem to diminish feminine identities or girls or women.

While not the last bastion of masculinity in America, wrestling remains an activity that can still be called "culturally male." Thus, wrestling stands as a relatively complete domain in which personal expression and team identification can be experienced in a male-specific context that still maintains, for the moment, the full support of the small but active adult wrestling community. It is within that world that the meanings and practices of masculinity are learned and carried out.

Chapter Three

Penile Implants

Embodying Medical Technology

Male identity itself often depends on a "functioning penis."[1] With age, the powers of the penis diminish for all men, and for some the functioning part of the penis wanes. Medical technology offers a solution, and I decided after various attempts with prescribed drugs to achieve and maintain an erection to go for the sure fix: a penile implant operation. The motivations for undergoing such a radical intervention surely are as varied as the men who decide to have this operation. In my case, the experience became fodder for my sociological imagination.

While research on embodiment relates various ways that people imagine their bodies and its parts (Waskul and Vannine 2006, Allen-Collinson and Owton 2015), fewer studies exist of the social penis, that is, of the imputed meanings and cultural contexts in which the penis is displayed and understood. Some feminist scholars consider the penis in order to identify the "mechanisms of effacement by which the specificity of the physical penis is obscured by a phallic ideal" (Stephens 2007, 85). By challenging phallocentric assumptions that underlie popular portrayals of the penis, feminists suggest that new meanings and relationships are possible. In other words, ideals about the potency of the penis are said to obscure the realities of it. Apparently, a close analysis is necessary to separate myth from reality.

In contemporary society, taboos against displaying and discussing "private" body parts have lessened. Consider such popular literature such as *The Little Book of Butts* and *The Little Book of Big Breasts* (Hansen 2012, 2013). Most pointedly, Dodsworth's (2017) book displays photographs of 100 penises, pictures accompanied by personal narratives that the men tell about themselves and their penises. These men relate the impact of early experiences, trauma and illness, anxieties, and even pride about how they think and feel about their penises. While her book intentionally eschews any theoretical analysis, the narratives accompanying each picture reveal the emotional connections that men have with this particular organ. In another book, Paley (1999) covers anatomy, preferences in size and shape among men and women, and the roles that the penis plays in popular culture and art. And, Miller (1995) offers a brief history of the penis in sports, fashion, and literature, emphasizing the role this organ plays in defining masculinity.

Underrepresented in all this literature is a symbolic interactionist analysis of the social penis. However, the notion that body parts take on meanings that are functionally related to core and peripheral values of a culture and practices of a society is commonplace in anthropology. For instance, early ethnological studies of penis sheaths suggests that this particular aspect of a society's material culture reveals functional interdependencies among institutions. The sheath may actually promote modesty and enable its wearer to control any spontaneity of the penis, such as an erection (Ucko, 1969).

Body parts have undergone analytic scrutiny. For example, Riem (1994) relates in detail her experiences, emotions, and consequences in her relationships with others due to losing her eye to cancer surgery. And, as Atkinson (2008) shows, men may resort to surgery to preserve or reinforce meanings of masculinity, and with the advance of surgical technology, repairs of and improvements upon body parts can be spectacular successes. For example, the re-attachment of a severed penis was recently accomplished by a surgical team in India (Krishnan, 2006). Also, the surgical practices developed for PIs have been applied to constructing penises for transgendered individuals (Rooker et al. 2019). This application is a medical means of reaffirming gender identity.

In her research with women who elected to have female genital cosmetic surgery, de Andrade (2010) draws out the connection between the motivations of women and market driven influences. She points to norms and images widely distributed through mass media that influence women's decisions to have such surgery. She also discusses ethical problems physicians face as they deal with possible ways to alter bodies.

Atkinson's (2006) study of men who have had facial surgery documents how, in an age of gender precarity, men privately and silently manage what they perceive as their shortfalls in meeting ideals of masculine appearance, while still achieving a modicum of control over it. While common supplements to the body such as glasses require less interactional work than surgical interventions, it appears that any altering of the biological body may call into question the social body. Ideals of appearance and medical procedures to achieve those ideals are conflated in the social meanings of the body.

Medical interventions often alter the body, sometimes permanently. For instance, Manderson and Stirling (2007) depict how women refer to the site of the mastectomy, and they examine the shifts in perspective that are indexed in the way women talk about this absent body part. Women may objectify the scar referring to "the breast" instead of "my breast," or even tattooing the scar to transform the absent breast into a part of the body.

Friedman (2001) documents using mythology, historical events, and changes in medical knowledge and practices how the relationship between man and his penis is often the key to a deep comprehension of epochs. Moving from ancient civilizations through changing conceptions of man and his penis, he identifies distinctive eras of the penis, from its roles in myths of the creation, through its demonization (the demon rod), its use to subjugate black men (the measuring stick), its role in psychoanalytic theories of nearly everything (the cigar), to the way scientific knowledge (both invalid and valid) changes the penis and its man. Friedman suggests that the penis is more than an organ: it is an idea that changes with history, as do all ideas of the body. However, at least in Western culture, understanding changes in the meanings of the penis can further understanding of culture in general.

According to Friedman, underlying meanings can be traced, however, to an ambiguous relationship between the man and his organ, a relationship that Friedman sees challenged by what he calls the erection industry (the industry built around the use of drugs, products, and procedures to enable an erection). In this article, I explore the aspects of the relationship between men and their organs by describing the changes that medicalization affects in awareness and practice after a penile implant.

PRIVATE PARTS

I use Bourdieu's concept of habitus to specify an aspect of what Weinberg and Williams (2010) call the looking glass body. They employ the concept of looking glass body in their study of the meanings of the naked body as related to sexual performance. I suggest that conceptualizing the body as social and consisting of at least a private parts habitus allows a symbolic interactionist perspective of the consequences of alterations of the penis.

I relate how penile implant surgery modifies and integrates into the looking glass body. Habitus as a device of this body refers to the physical embodiment of cultural capital, to the deeply ingrained habits, skills, and dispositions that we have acquired through life experiences in a particular social and cultural nexus. Habitus allows for and enables the navigation of social worlds. And, since it exists in a reciprocal relationship with "objective" social structure, understanding the particular aspects of a given habitus and its functions permits extrapolation to structures and back to situations. The concept has been applied to an astonishing array of subjects from cars (Sheller 2007), barbershop singers (Nash 2012), linguistic practices (Jones 2001) and even feces (Weinberg and Williams 2005).

A private parts habitus refers to meaning and practices associated with intimate anatomy that accumulate over one's lifetime, and that reflect sexual history and eccentricities. Of course, there can be variation within this habitus. For example, while Dodsworth's (2017) book centers on the penis, its main message ranges outward to stories of sexual conquest, failures, embarrassment, and bragging rights. Clearly, men develop an understanding of what this part of their self means and what they can and cannot do with it. Ambiguity and or crisis in this habitus is implicated in decisions to have penile implant surgery.

A private parts habitus is embodied in institutional meanings and societal structures at the macro level and in a concept of body at the micro. Since childhood, boys learn to conceal their penis, display it in situationally appropriate ways, and, most importantly, to treat the penis as private. These social practices and the meanings that one gives the penis can have medical meanings, or as Friedman suggests, a crisis of the penis and a medical response to this crisis has lead to the erection industry. A patient, hence, has a well-established private parts habitus that remains largely tacit whenever he visits a urologist, for example. Impotency creates a crisis within the private parts habitus. What follows are narratives of that crisis that illustrate the linkages among meanings and practices.

Medicalizing the Penis

A symbolic interactionist perspective can augment the medical model. By conceptualizing the habitus as one of many cognitive and emotional devices for creating what Weinberg and Williams (2010) call a looking glass body, by which we mean the interpretations and emotional reaction that an actor makes of his or her body within the imaginations of judgment of others.

The medical model begins when a patient seeks a physician's help for his impotence. The physician typically pays little attention to the patient's private parts habitus. I recall being asked no questions about how I think about my penis. After diagnosis, the physician describes possible causes, but he or she moves quickly to detailed accounts of remedies. By overlaying the looking glass body and its device, the private parts habitus, on the experience of having penile implant, I intend to understand the personal and social consequences of penile implant surgery. Whereas the medical model emphasizes outcomes, the SI model highlights meanings.

All manner of human fragilities, from drug abuse to deformities, have been transformed into medical problems that purportedly have solutions which are

devoid of stigma and thoroughly normalized. Such is the case with male impotency. Impotency, in everyday life meanings, goes beyond the dysfunction
of an organ to the man himself. When we say a man is impotent, we degrade
him, and, as the word suggests, we see him as having lost power in some
sense. Men who experience impotency often experience challenges to their
self-esteem and sense of worth. Impotency, we might say, shatters the looking glass body. Impotency may become a stigma, but since it is not public, it
discredits only in private or intimate interactions. Goffman (1963) might have
called it a stealth stigma had he analyzed impotency, since it is invisible in
public interaction. Of course, as a cause of more visible manifestations, such
as depression or irascibility, impotence, if uncovered in interaction, impotency could be a stigma. Some people who have used online dating services
for mature adults report that potential partners may discuss sexual activity.
Thus, neutralizing stigma becomes necessary for continuing the relationship
(personal interview).

The condition of impotency, especially in older men, has ramifications
that affect self-concept, and, certainly, relationships not only with intimate
partners but with others as well. A study of the expectations men with ED
have before treatment shows that relationships with partners is an important
consideration in choosing a treatment and that expected outcomes include
increased quality of life (Henninger, Höhn, Leiber, and Berner 2015).

Therefore, impotence, once seen as character weakness or even the consequence of immoral and lascivious habits, is discussed in the medical model in
anatomical and metric terms, and medical technological interventions are the
main resources for restoration and normalization and stigmatic neutralization
(Friedman 2001).

The vast literature on the medical model covers an array of illnesses and
dysfunctions (Conrad 1992, 2005, Conrad and Schneider 1992), but there are
few detailed narratives about the penis. Critiques of the medical model do
exist: for instance, Tiefer (1994) refers to phallocentrism (the assumption that
it is possible to achieve the perfect erection through medical intervention) as
detrimental to appreciating the full range of degrees of erections and the accommodation that partners make to these variations. His critique implies that
couples can have pleasure with a partially erect penis. However, correctives
such as his to the medical model are rare and remain outside the scope of the
medical model of the penis.

The medical model begins with the physician's assumption that the patient
had at one time a "normal" sex life. Whatever that life might be is irrelevant,
since the physician uses this assumption as a starting point for diagnosis. Usually, this amounts to a brief account of the cause of impotency. The causes
of impotence, are richly depicted, running the gamut from traumas such as

automobile accidents, sports injuries, to diseases of various kinds, most typically those that restrict the flow of blood to the penis. However, regardless of
the cause, attention shifts quickly to remedies, glossing over the details of a
man's private parts habitus.

Knowledge and description of the remedies for impotence is rich and
detailed in the medical model. These remedies vary from pharmaceutical to
elaborate accounts of surgery. In the case of penile implant surgery, one can
find descriptions of the surgical procedures, even a video showing an actual
operation, and one demonstrating how to use the penile pump. Most of these
websites are sponsored by physicians or businesses that manufacture the
devices. They are technical, professional in tone, and devoid of any erotic
content.

Penile implants (PI) have been available as a treatment for erectile dysfunction since the 1970s. There are several types of implants, but the most
popular uses a reservoir implanted in the abdomen, a pump inserted in the
scrotum and inflatable tubes implanted on either side of the penis. While no
accurate count exists for the number of men in the United States who have an
implant, PI is a common treatment for men for whom pharmaceutical treat-
ments have proven ineffective, and for those with erectile dysfunction (ED)
as a condition resulting from some health issue. Cases of ED are increasing
in the United States, with an estimated 30 million men with the condition.
There are several causes for ED, some of them linked to obesity and arterial
diseases, others to diabetic conditions or trauma. For example, some causes
of ED include Peyronie's disease, side effects of prostate surgery, and even
reaction to medications.

With the introduction of ED medicines such as Viagra and Cialis, the percentage of patients electing to have the surgery has declined (Smart, CNN,
June 23, 2015). Still, the procedure is considered one of the most "successful"
of all operations. Surveys have reported impressively high patient satisfaction
with the outcome of the surgery Generally, a consistent 90 percent of patients
and their partners report they are satisfied or happy with their implants; that
they have resumed intercourse within weeks of the surgery; and that they are
largely satisfied with the surgical result (Bettocchi et al. 2009, Carvalheira,
Santana, and Pereira 2015). These surveys gloss over the details that constitute satisfaction and leave unexplored the interactional impact that a technological intervention to the genitals can have.

I relate aspects of my own account of male impotence and those of men
who post comments at websites devoted to such discussions to supplement
and enrich the medical model with lived-through meanings. At the forefront
of the analysis is the sense that men make of the "problem," and how a
private parts habitus is modified and maintained. While the medical model

minimizes the patient's private parts habitus, emphasizing technical and anatomical features of the penis, an SI narrative considers the significance of the surgery for the nature and character of the habitus even though the medical narrative frames the overall process.

My Method

My own experience of ED and my decision to have a penile implant provided an opportunity to describe the private parts habitus in general and my own, specifically (see Riemer 1977). After several visits to my family physician, I learned the reason for my ED was probably circulatory—plaque somewhere in the system. I was referred to a urologist who specialized in PI surgery who encouraged me to read and think about the having the procedure done. I began to ponder my private parts habitus and to imagine the accommodations my wife and I would have to make to the implant. I offer here an account of some aspects of my experience of having an implant. I depict how interpretations of the meanings of penile implants for those who receive them function to become part of the "natural" body and even augment the physiology of male genitalia. In a sense, this analysis rests on my experience with this transformative process, but it pushes observational opportunities to a degree that collapses the distance between observer and observed—what might be called an "extreme" form of participant observation.

However, as Becker (2017) writes, sociologists have long used their own experiences as evidence for concepts and theories. Roth (1963) turned his tuberculosis into an opportunity to test sociological concepts. Roy (1952) used his job in a machine shop to create evidence for generalizations about how workers organized their time on the line.

While my method is primarily participatory, similar to such works as Murphy's *The Body Silent* (1987), I also follow what Anderson (2006) calls analytic auto-ethnography, which emphasizes that personal experiences be grounded in a sense of membership (here, men with penile implants), one's presence in the text, reflexive analysis, and a commitment to situating one's experiences within an abstract set of concepts that permit sociological insights. Hence, as I recall experiences, look at notes, and reconstruct events, I do so as patient and sociologist. I undergo surgery that alters my taken-for-granted understandings of my private body parts and of at least some aspects of my social self.

How the Transformation Starts

The decision to have implant surgery follows a process. While I identity this process from my own experience, other men describe it similarly. First, there is a disruption or breach in the private parts habitus resulting from a variety of sources. Then a period, usually fairly lengthy, of various remedies for ED. These remedies, while successful for many, do not work for all men. In fact, the "success" rates for ED drugs are often greatly exaggerated in popular understandings. As the following quote suggests, while there are many causes of impotency and in remedies tried, for a man who decides to have PI surgery, there is a recognition that remedies are not working and the hope of some for some restoration gone. So, one must have a "come to Jesus" moment," that is, face the biological reality that one will never again have a "natural erection."

> I am 59 years old and have had ED for about 6 years. Probably a side effect of my diabetes type II. Have tried the pills and that was great for a few years but kind of expensive. After that it was pump [reference to a mechanical device] which worked but was damn trouble having to stop the flow of love making to pump up the penis. Tried shots but I could not get past sticking my penis with a needle. It is just not natural and I did not get a real good erection and now take Cialis 5 mg daily and use the pump. it works but there had to be something out there that was better. I had a come to Jesus meeting with my Uro and we discussed all the pros and cons of the implants. Based on his information and talking to the guy on Frank TALK, I have decided to go ahead and get the implant this fall. that in a nutshell is my story. (User losangeles, 2013)

THE MEDICAL EXAMINATION

The pre-operative examinations for PI surgery bear similarities to the emotional management and de-eroticization that Emerson (1970) describes in her on observations of such examinations. Just as doctors and nurses follow routines of action and speech that are aimed to take any sexual intent or meaning out of a gynecological examination, so do the doctors and nurses who specialize in PI surgery and treatment. Matter-of-fact speech is used, along with technical terms to relate to the patient what will happen in the operation and what consequences might ensue.

For example, after a discussion of the way a penile pump works and how mechanisms of ejaculation remain unaffected, a lengthy warning about the percentages of cases involving infections, and answers to questions about the effects on the glans (will it engorge post PI operation?), the doctor looks solemnly at me and says, "Now, let's look IN your penis." After the shock of the "IN," he proceeds to do just that. The examination includes an internal manual check of the prostate and a look for abnormalities; and, after the doctor's decision that surgery is a possibility, there is a consultation between doctor and patient. Sometimes the patient requests a few days or weeks to "think about it." Finally, a mutual doctor-patient agreement is made (a come to Jesus moment) and a date for surgery is set. In my examinations, my wife accompanied me and took part in all discussions.

The Surgery

The experience of surgery as a social form remains a relatively unexplored domain. Millions of people around the world have "had surgery." In the United States, it is a highly routinized experience with preoperative procedures that include the creation of a "case" and "charts," all of which can be understood as the construction of a medical entity, that is, a person becoming socialized as a patient (cf. Parsons 1951, Arluke, Kennedy and Kessler 1979, Perry 2011). Surgery transforms the status and identity that one brings to the hospital, and thereby one loses most, if not all, of their previous social identities. A patient may also have high social status, for instance, be a physician or another kind of "very important person," but while these statuses may affect when and where a surgery is scheduled and whether a particular surgeon performs the procedure and other perks associated with high status, "surgery" as a social form governs the experience. Of course, surgeries vary from saving life to cosmetic alterations of facial features, and considerations such as the ethnicity, race, or gender of the patient do influence, sometimes dramatically, social contexts that accompany undergoing a surgery.

In the case of an alteration of male private parts, the experience of surgery is not distinctive from other forms of surgery. The check-in is the same, as with any surgery that requires an overnight stay, protocols govern virtually each step leading to the surgery itself. I point out the ordinary nature of the preliminaries for having PI surgery to contrast the extraordinary effect it has on altering the "private parts" habitus.

Out, Damned Catheter

After the operation, coming out of recovery and upon awaking from the night in the hospital with all that it entails (blood pressure checks, sleep interruptions from nurses), I saw two young women standing at my bedside. One of them cheerfully announced that they were there to remove the catheter which had been in place since the surgery. That they did, grabbing my penis with one hand and pulling the catheter out with the other. Such pain I have rarely experienced!

I was able to walk a little and joke with my wife about my hopefully temporary predicament, but the swelling of my scrotum was nothing short of specular. When I asked about whether this was normal, a nurse claimed that she has seen them the size of a basketball. Some patients, she added, swell very little. Well, I suppose my set of black and very large "balls" (grapefruit size) were somewhere near average. I was only slightly relieved.

Furthermore, not disclosed in the preliminaries leading to surgery was that the procedure included a deliberate puncture of my huge, blackened scrotum, which for several days bled a steady drip, soaking several pads a day. Of course, this "drain hole" was there to minimize swelling. Still, keeping the swelling under control required ice packs and soaks in the bath tub. These soaks in the bath were particularly memorable since the water was often tinged with blood. At this point, thoughts about sexual activity were remote, and I hoped for at least a return to a normal scrotum. With a bruised penis and a huge leaking scrotum, my private parts habitus had been severely transformed.

Over the next few weeks, my penis and scrotum slowly returned to normal sizes and colors. My private parts habitus slowly re-emerged, as I recognized shape and feel of my "normal" penis, that is, according to my preoperative private parts habitus. Several months later, after I had more or less fully recovered, I saw my family care physician for an annual checkup. He asked how the surgery went, and I asked him if he would like to see the picture of my swollen scrotum. He thought for a minute and said, "Yeah, that might be helpful for talking with other men who might consider having this surgery." I showed him the picture my wife had taken in the hospital. His eyes widened and he said, "I haven't seen anything like that since I worked on a cadaver in medical school."

Total recovery from the surgery took quite some time and required some serious rethinking about what one's scrotum should feel like. Since the pump mechanism inside my scrotum now has become a "third ball," the habitus must change. Within two to three weeks after surgery, it is possible to pump up the penis. However, since lingering swelling can last several months, the very thought of squeezing the bulb to achieve an erection does little to evoke erotic images. And since the entire scrotum has been recently bruised, pumping up can turn the skin of the scrotum blue. Furthermore, since patients sometimes have trouble learning how to pump, return trips to the doctor's office might be necessary. I will describe my visits in connection with my discussion of de-erotic techniques employed by physicians and nurses.

As time passes and swelling goes down, normal skin tone appears and thoughts of a resumed sex life, the primary reason for the ordeal, return. Penetration for the first-time, post-surgery, can be a thrilling and quite satisfactory episode for both partners. During foreplay, for me, there were moments of doubt as to whether the penis is "hard" enough" to penetrate, and whether or not I had mastered the technique of achieving full inflation (erection). In the case of my wife and I, the first try was successful and even joyous, as we laughed and welcomed the return of our "previous sex life."

The return of the "rod," as Friedman (2001) might say, can be a marker for the reestablished habitus. Eventually, perhaps six months post-surgery, the pump becomes a "natural" part of one's anatomy, and the outline of the pump can be felt as can the valve for deflating the penis after sex. The bulb can be moved around within the scrotum, and squeezing it to inflate the penis no longer makes one squeamish. In fact, so does squeezing the penis become "normal," as does the low squishing sound produced by fluid passing from tubes in the penis, back to the reservoir.

De-Erotic Techniques

A private parts habitus enables various interpretations of touches of the genitalia from scratching and masturbation to the erotic. And, whenever a medical procedure requires touching some part of the genitalia, as Emerson (1970) documented, de-eroticizing techniques convert private meanings into medical. Some of these techniques include: settings (medical offices, standardized decorum, medical equipment, and relatively sterile and officious ambiance), use of the patient's surname, uniform dress among the medical staff, and requiring the patient to wear a gown. Controlling gaze is another technique used by medical staff.

This involves not only minimal eye contact but facial expressions and body language that neutralizes any possible erotic meanings. Touches are brief, glove-covered, and mechanical. In one instance, post-surgery, I was having difficulty inflating the tubes to achieve an erection. Inflating or pumping up entails grasping the bulb that is now inside the scrotum and squeezing. Since that entire area is sensitive after the surgery and since squeezing the bulb always necessitates squeezing the skin of the scrotum, learning to accomplish an erection requires a little practice. The bulb is slippery and the bulb sometimes "air locks," which means it is necessary to squeeze hard to move the air bubble out of the bulb. I had to return to the doctor's office twice in order to ensure that the mechanism was operating properly. Both times I was assigned a female nurse who had a reputation of being skilled at helping patients learn "pumping up." She entered the examination room, requested that I drop my pants (no gown this time), then quickly and mechanically, without looking me in the eye, seized the bulb and, with a decisive forefinger to thumb, squeezed to demonstrate the proper technique for inflating.

The doctor then entered the room and suggested that when I become comfortable with the pumping up technique that that technique could become part of mine and my partner's foreplay rituals. He and his nurse were offering advice about how to reconfigure a private parts habitus so that the mechanical procedure can replace or substitute for the organic arousal stage of foreplay. Subsequently, I learned that before that can happen, the technique must become effortless and distracting "airlocks" must be cleared well before foreplay starts. Such an incorporation of medical technology into foreplay never happened for my wife and me, though we made other accommodations, especially on the part of my wife.

Throughout these post-operative visits to the doctor's office, the use of medical jargon and references to studies and results from experience also function to de-erotize the meanings associated with discussing private parts. By allusion, however, common-sense, everyday knowledge was acknowledged by the doctor, for example, he referred to variation in penis size among patients and pointed out that the devices themselves are designed to accommodate variation. The tubes that are inserted on both sides of the penis during the operation come in different sizes. Such discussions with reference to the pros and cons of the different types of PI devices (Coloplast Titan, AMS 700, non-inflatable, AMS Ambicor), the results of patients' satisfaction surveys peppered with medical terms such as glans and prosthesis, can be quite effective in de-erotizing any conversation about one's private parts.

Reconfiguring the Private Parts Habitus

The meanings carried within habitus have a relative permanency, particularly since their enactment reinforces and turns social structures into capital (Wacquant 2016, 70). As the term itself suggests, habits and deeply rooted cultural tropes, reinforced by everyday applications, result in firmly established ways of making sense of, in this case, one's male genitalia. When an alteration occurs, as is the case with PI, the habitus must accommodate. Describing the ways that accommodation takes place illustrates both the flexibility and the permanence of core meanings. In other words, the habitus is so persistent that it endures in ways that allow the cultural tropes to continue. For example, if a man were particularly proud of the length of his penis, and penis length is a cultural trope in mass entertainment and common-sense knowledge, he must re-interpret what the loss of length means. As I will illustrate later, men can be creative, misogynistic, or simply insensitive in their interpretations.

Irrevocable changes in the size and shape of the penis result from PI surgery. Both girth and length of the penis are, post-PI, determined by the tubes and what is left of the corpus cavernosum, (columns of tissue running along the sides of the penis) and the corpus spongiosum (a column of sponge-like tissue running along the front of the penis and ending at the glans). Since the anatomy of the penis has been altered and these components are central to a "natural" erection, there can be no "natural" erection, and the girth of the penis is slightly less. Of course, "slightly less" in an objective sense can be "much less" in the private parts habitus. Many men seem to be bothered by this effect of the PI, as this is often mentioned in online chat and discussion groups.

After PI surgery, the penis must be re-thought. Most men consider these losses to be more than compensated by a functioning penis. After recovery from the surgery, most men report that they soon regain that "old feeling," especially after a successful ejaculation. During sexual arousal, they report having sensations of a natural erection. This is partly the result of the glans enlarging and of the well-established linkage between the brain and penis that triggers a natural erection. Whatever the "natural" connection, in the reformed habitus, these sensations become "natural" in the sense that they form the essences of a reconstructed habitus.

In addition to the altered feeling of arousal, there are other changes to the anatomy of the penis that require interpretation. A flaccid penis becomes a deflated penis, and an erect penis no longer stands upright, but sticks straight out from the body. Pumping up replaces the spontaneous arousal. And, there is feeling of having a "hybrid dick," that is, of being able to feel the flexible plastic tubes on either side of the shaft, which when deflated, feel as if they are kinked like a garden hose. According to online sources, partners mention the altered feel of the shaft (*Frank Talk* 2018). They report learning to accept "new" sensations as "ordinary" when caressing and simulating the penis. One modification mentioned by a partner had to do with recognizing when her partner was "truly" aroused. In "normal" foreplay, the penis shaft becomes tumescent to a degree that is obvious to the person stimulating it. However, with a PI, the shaft is non-responsive to stimulation; hence, a partner must rely on communicative cues and sensing the slight enlargement of the glans. The period of adjustment to this change is typically short, though in some cases, it may become a problematic feature of the foreplay routine between a couple. In my search of the chat rooms, discussion boards, and literature, I saw no mention of the long-term effects of this modification of the penis.

Routinization plays a crucial role in normalizing effects of the PI. Most men report that within a few months of the operation, after healing is complete, the "feel" of the device becomes more "natural": there is less of a feel of artificiality. Still, sitting and sleeping in certain positions provokes a reminder that "it's industrial" down there. Essentially, the bulb is a third "ball," located in the scrotum: a presence that requires consideration while crossing one's legs. In due time, the apparatus transforms into something natural in the habitus: it becomes "mine" and simply is.

Also, to be considered is the situation of "public" display. By this I mean whenever daily routines such as exercise at the gym, hunting trips, or whatever occasion might require showering in front of other men, one must be sure that the penis is completely deflated in order to appear non-sexual, that is, flaccid. Since the penis can no longer shrink and since daily movements, especially rigorous exercise, can cause some fluid to enter the shafts resulting in a semi-erect penis, it is necessary to deflate it regularly to avoid embarrassing situations.

In one case, an informant remarks, half-jokingly, that he is troubled that his "new" penis leans to the "right," which is contrary to his political inclinations. While this seems a trivial concern, it illustrates just some of the necessary changes required for the habitus to routinize and de-problematize the appearance of the penis.

Another aspect of public display is deciding to whom to talk about having had the operation. Do you tell family members or friends about the PI surgery? I did tell some friends about it, one who had had PI surgery himself and another, a physician, both in presumed confidence. However, in the case of family members who knew I had had an operation, my wife and I referred to it as hernia surgery. In other words, I maintained my previous self-presentation through lying (Cf. Sacks 1975).

The Looking Glass Penis

Charles H. Cooley's (1922) concept of the looking glass self suggests that our images of ourselves are formed from our imagination of how we think and feel about how others think and feel about us. Weinberg and Williams (2010) apply the concept to the nude body. Their research focuses on how partners think and feel about their naked bodies during sex, that is, how they imagine their partners evaluate their bodies. They find that the looking glass body is directly related to more general assessments about the meanings of sex. For example, more positive images of one's body are associated with a greater variety of sexual activities, and among women, negative or self-critical attitudes about their nude bodies are restrictive of sexual practices.

PI surgery alters the looking glass body. While "objectively" a sex partner or a shower buddy might not even notice, nor care to glance at the naked penis, this does not mean that the habitus is unaffected. As indicated above, there are many changes that must be refigured both literally and within the mind (cf. G. H. Mead 1934). Following Cooley (1922) here is a sketch of the looking glass penis:

> My imagination of how I think my penis appears to others, both as an intimate and as a "public" appearance.
> My imagination of how others evaluate this appearance of my penis.
> My emotional reaction to that imagined evaluation.

To add descriptive to the concept of the looking glass penis, consider the matter of size. Research shows variation in size and appearance of the penis

(Veale et al. 2014). Furthermore, an "objective" study of how women think about penis size (Prause 2015) shows that women may vary in what they prefer in penis size, according to whether they image an encounter with one in a one-night stand or a long-term relationship. For example, the women in the sample of this study preferred a larger penis for a casual encounter and one only slightly larger than average for a long-term relationship.

In contrast to this "objective" reporting, consider what a man imagines his partner's view of the appearance of his penis to be. He may think of himself as small or large, and he may project this image onto his partner's view. The insight that interactionism contributes to such an understanding is that it is what the man thinks his partner thinks that shapes the private parts habitus. If a man images that others (intimate and public) see him as "large," he may be dissatisfied with the loss of both girth and length from the surgery. Likewise, if he is "small," then the surgery may exacerbate the perspective of being small. If there are other irregularities in the penis or scrotum, the possible concerns become more complex.

When a man imagines how his appearance is evaluated by others, he may see the decrease in size as irrelevant, since his partner never mentions it. Also, he may limit exposure to the public by avoiding showering at the gym, or managing his exposure through the use of a towel or robe. On the other hand, the tubes in the shaft of the penis prevent a fully flaccid penis and a man may imagine that he appears "larger" than he was preoperatively. Hence, he may be even bolder or less reluctant to expose his "public" penis.

The emotional reaction to altered genitalia may range from "what do I care" to "you should be so lucky." Generally, survey data following PI surgery indicate that men are quite satisfied and quickly establish a "normal" private-parts habitus (Carvalheira, Santana, and Pereira 2015). In other words, the management of exposure and the meanings of intimacy become normalized through routine and acceptance, even if imagined.

When Technology Fails: Disembodiment

Even a brief visit to chat rooms where PI surgery is discussed reveals that there are circumstances in which PI surgery might be considered a failure. These outcomes and the sense that men make of them are typically due to general poor health, problematic relationships with partners, or even a fatalistic stance toward aging. While these interpretations of the consequences of the surgery are fairly uncommon (less than 10 percent of all PI surgery), they do reveal another way to make sense of the experiences.

> I got my implant several years ago and have always had problems with it. Got an infection and had to have it removed and then re-implanted. My partner is

not much interested in sex anymore, and frankly, if I have any more infections, I'll just get the thing out and forget about it. (*Frank Talk*, 2017)

We have no information about how this man's partner thinks and feels about this situation. Our chat room friend, however, clearly has a fatalistic view of the whole matter. Emphatically, I agree that enduring PI surgery more than once with a less than enthusiastic sex partner could well lead one to wish for dispensing altogether with the pain and the troublesome aspects of intimate relationships. However, even though the PI can be removed, the reconfiguration of the habitus has already happened and PI surgery continues as a lingering influence on the habitus. In this particular case, I image this man being reminded of the ordeal each time he touches or looks at his permanently limp penis.

CONCLUSION

Both medically and socially, PI surgery requires a rethinking of what constitutes a normal penis. The normalization process outlined in this article traces the meanings of a penis through erectile dysfunction, medical remedial steps, to the decision to have surgery, through the experiences associated with surgery, and to the subsequent modifications of a private parts habitus.

Bourdieu (1984) intended his concept of habitus to strengthen a theoretical understanding of the articulation between individual and society (Wacquant 2016). Bourdieu encouraged researchers to seek out the connections between various forms of capital (economic and cultural) and the details of individual actions (for example, taste in food and clothing). In this way, a sociologist may explicate fully the reciprocal influences of social forces. The depiction of a private parts habitus uncovers interrelationships among individual understandings of body parts and reveals the embodiment of medical interventions. In the case of PI surgery, this relationship results in a normalization of the PI device as it becomes a routine part of the habitus. The habitus accommodates the structures of medical practice into the meanings of the social penis and more general the looking glass body.

The embodiment process described here may be prescient of other technological interventions such as bionic prosthetic legs and hands. The malleability of self-awareness and its accommodation to radical changes demonstrated in this analysis may extend to the merger of technology and biology. I suggest that understanding changes in the private parts habitus may contribute to understanding how technology and biology interact. In particular, the testimony of partners and the experiences related by men who have undergone the PI procedure demonstrate the resiliency of habitus. That familiar feeling of normality is deeply imbedded in a wide variety of experiences and meanings that together become part of important intimate relationships.

NOTES

1. Parts of this chapter were previously published in *Qualitative Sociological Review* XVII, no. 2 (2021): 88–102.

Part II

The two chapters in Part Two deal with humor and how it intersects with a variety of social forces. The comparison of two TV sitcoms broadcasted thirty years apart shows how conceptions of race, class, and gender reflect changes that mirror a larger shift in society from modern to postmodern meanings. Between the heydays of *All in the Family* and that of *Curb Your Enthusiasm*, the way people talk about race and the presentation of race have changed dramatically. My view of these sit-coms goes into details of talk and self-presentation, and suggests that humor is mutable and responsive to social change.

Chapter Six relates my experiences in teaching a class on humor to an elderly group of students enrolled in a course that was part of a lifetime learning program for retired folks. While I did not envision this chapter as an extension of my examination of sit-com humor, I realized that my effort to teach furtive sociology does underscore and follow interconnections: race, class, gender, geography (urban/rural), and a consideration of age. Chapter Six, then, can be read as an elaboration of the social aspects of humor, ranging from the inklings of standup comedy in vaudeville to feminists' critiques of gender hierarchies, to the racially sensitive humor of modern standup comedians.

Chapter Four

Archie, Meet Larry

*Framing Race in Two
Acclaimed Television Comedy Series*

When I was a grade school kid, television sets became affordable for most American families.[1] I did not grow up in poverty, but my family was by no means wealthy. So, when we finally purchased a TV, my father did not want me to tell my friends at school that we had a TV. Perhaps he did not want me to brag, or maybe he was afraid his decision to get a TV would be seen as poor money management by our neighbors? I will never know his reasons. All I remember is that I was excited about having a TV. I remember when I was given permission to turn it on for the first time, and thrill of seeing a commercial for termite control slowly emerge from the darkened screen. I was literally "dying to tell" someone my family's good fortune.

So, on the playground at recess, I disobeyed my father and told a girl whom I barely knew, the glorious news. We have a TV. She was not only unimpressed but having already mastered the put down, she replied: We've had a TV for over a year. That burned into my long-term memory and probably helped establish in my sociological imagination the importance of understanding the impact of mass media.

Popular television programs reflect and shape public discourse. Over the course of 30 years, encompassing the Civil Rights era to present day "reality" and "in your face" comedy television, what is said about race and to members of races has undergone remarkable changes. This paper identifies some of those changes, as characterized by two popular television programs, *All in the Family* and *Curb Your Enthusiasm*. Archie Bunker's malapropisms (from *All in the Family*) and the sarcastic and sardonic everyday life experiences of Larry David (from *Curb Your Enthusiasm*) document broader issues of race in America. These programs provide a snapshot of transformations in discourse about race and bookend the consequences of changes in television over the period. As television morphed from network hegemony to competitive, multi-channeled programming, discourse about race, as least in comedic context, mirrors the restraints and freedoms of these changes.

Lazarsfeld and Merton (1948) were among the first to point out that images, particularly those embedded in compelling narratives, may be major influences in public policy on controversial issues. For example, Lipsitz (1986, 357) shows how early television situation comedies were "charged with special responsibility for making new economic and social relations credible and legitimate to audiences haunted by ghosts from the past." These comedies did this by introducing a framework and a vocabulary for transitioning from class and ethnic identities to consumerist ones.

Lipsitz pointed out that *Mama* was framed as Norwegian nostalgia, *The Goldbergs* as Jews in the Bronx, *Amos 'n Andy* as Blacks in Harlem, *Life with Luigi* as Italians in Chicago, *Hey, Jeannie* as Irish in Brooklyn, and *Life with Riley* as working-class migrants in Los Angeles. In all these portrayals, the tensions and problems of strong ethnic/racial identity were resolved through membership in a society driven by commodification, that is, by acquiring purchasing power in a consumerist economy. After 1958, television networks shifted their focus to suburban consumers and the new middle class. Television, hence, shifted focus with the flow of expendable income from the city to the suburbs, as ethnic identity faded or became, as Gans (1979) put it, symbolic.

Vera and Gordon (2003) review how race, particularly whiteness, has been presented in the movies. They suggest that we live in a "cinematic society, one that presents and represents itself through movie and television screens [and that] the social organization of cinematic societies is dramatically different from that of non-cinematic ones" (Vera and Gordon, 8–9). American movies, they write, have celebrated whiteness in ways that helped globalize racism. In *Men in Black*, released in 1997, for example, a Black hero represents a common "new" identity of saviors of the world, which the authors show, is rooted in a conception of whiteness.

Occasionally, a portrayal of race strikes a raw nerve of anxiety, fear, or even hope. We recognize these portrayals through public reaction to them, such as the reaction to the movie, *Birth of a Nation* (1915). For the first generation of the twentieth century, *Birth of a Nation* embodied white resistance to what seemed an inevitable wave of social change in black and white relationships. And, later, during the Civil Rights era, the movie, *Guess Who's Coming to Dinner?* (1967), dealt with interracial marriage in a way that reinforced a moral and emotional interpretation of miscegenation. As mass media audiences grew and as the media extended their reach through the popularity of movies and later, television, producers, and writers were emboldened to tackled racial controversy through serious drama and comedy.

Still, as a large body of literature on race and television comedy attests, race in the popular media is framed or channeled (Hamamoto 1989, Guerrero 1993, Gray 1995, Rocchio 2000, Hunt 2005, Nadel 2005) in ways that simultaneously express aspirations, frustrations, and restraints. In media representation of cultural differences, "there remains a contradictory character, one where the leaks, fractures, tensions, and contradictions in a stratified, multicultural society continue to find expression" (Hunt 2005, 171).

Hamamoto's (1989) early book showed that the subject of race became a channel for ideologically framing national issues; and, Nadel (2005) has recently extended an analysis of race on television to include how mutable race categories shift with international and national social policies and practices. Black and white distinctions, he suggests, are portrayed within such broader contexts as the cold war, corporate images of the future, program development driven by consumer preferences and social movements. Nadel (2005) writes that the era when television can shape a national identity may be coming to an end when, instead of a national audience, "we have a nation of fragments" (185).

In the era of the Civil Rights movement, *Guess Who's Coming to Dinner?* garnered praise from critics and criticism from the NAACP. While the film legitimized interracial marriage, it placed serious limitations on such marriages by depicting "eligible partners" as virtually "ideal" mates, save for their race. Generally, media scholars seem to agree that there are discourse domains that operate in the framing of race, especially on television. Some of these domains include the assimilationist, rendering race invisible; the pluralist or separate-but-equal, following a cultural tendency to distance racial differences categorically; and the multicultural tendency that heralds a new social order.

As demonstrated by Wasko and others (Wasko 2005), television attempts to juggle the presentation of race in ways that do not repel viewers or the commercial backing that funds the shows. Discourse domains about race clearly are shaped by these tensions. The characters of Archie Bunker and Larry David represent two distinctive eras of television (network and cable). The following deconstruction of the characters reveals transformations in race discourse that promote the understanding of "leaks, fractures and contradictions" to which Hunt and others allude.

In 1971, *All in the Family*, introduced American television viewers to a bigot. Archie Bunker, a working-class, uneducated, irascible white male was given a forum to speak about all sorts of social issues, not the least of which was race prejudice. The program garnered awards, critical acclaim, and wide-spread popularity.

What is "funny" about Archie is how he persists in his thinking even when the audience and he are shown how wrong he is in each situation. Archie, a pompous comedic figure who, at every opportunity, makes racial slurs, embodies negative and naïve views of race. Through an unpacking of the Archie Bunker character, an interpretation of "proper" views of race unfolds. This comedy series which appeared on network television for nine seasons and aired over 200 episodes, provides a wealth of materials for answering questions about portrayals of race prejudice during the 1970s.

At this writing, 60 adroitly interrelated episodes of *Curb Your Enthusiasm* have been aired since its premier in October of 2000. The show is produced from an outline without a script giving it an unrehearsed, in the moment spontaneity. Many of the actors are real-life friends and professional peers, and Larry David has enlisted directors who have sensibilities similar to his own (a majority of the episodes have been directed by Robert B. Weide). The characters, dialogues, and stories in this series suggest that this particular framing of everyday life stands as an exemplar of quotidian sensibilities in a contemporary context, and in particular, interpretations of race.

The writer and main character of *Curb Your Enthusiasm* is Larry David, who also wrote and produced, along with Jerry Seinfeld, the successful sitcom series, *Seinfeld*. Not only did *Seinfeld* command a massive audience, it won critical acclaim, garnering an Emmy Award for Outstanding Comedy Series, a Peabody Award for Best Television Entertainment, a Golden Globe Award for Best TV Series, Comedy/Musical, and a Screen Actors Guild Award for Outstanding Ensemble Performance in a Comedy Series.

In *Curb Your Enthusiasm*, Larry David plays himself, a character of interest, given the success of the *Seinfeld* show. *Seinfeld* vaulted Larry David into riches, and the series depicts Larry's hilariously awkward lifestyle of encounters with strangers, family, and friends. *Curb Your Enthusiasm* is a "verité-style footage of David (playing himself) at home, at work and around town, as he gets into predicaments with fictional and real-life personalities" (HBO, 2006).

Curb Your Enthusiasm carries on the *Seinfeld* tradition. It puts Larry David in a variety of situations in which he stubbornly persists in his definition of the situation, particularly in racialized encounters. This awkward juxtaposition of Larry's definitions of the situation and those of the characters he encounters, and the fact that the characters talk freely, the way they might in real life, gives the successful show a spicy street-talking edge.

All in the Family and *Curb Your Enthusiasm* represent distinct eras in the portrayal of race relations, and in the transformation of television from three networks that market to the common dominator, to niche marketing. *All in the Family*, a network show relying on the sale of commercial time, takes a sanctimonious and highly judgmental stance toward race prejudice. This stance embodies a simplistic conception of prejudice, humanized through the Archie Bunker character whose negative attitudes about race are blatant.

Curb Your Enthusiasm, in contrast, offers a complex and multidimensional conception of prejudice, humanized by the character of Larry David, whose blunders stem from trying too hard to get race right. *Curb Your Enthusiasm* is a Home Box Office production that aims for smaller audiences in the cable market. Still, comparisons of the two portrayals suggest that 1) conceptions of race have shifted in the United States since *All in the Family* from fixed, definitional, and "individualized" contents towards situational, fluid, and ironic ones; 2) this shift parallels transformations in American society in the entertainment industry from network domination to niche marketing, in patterns of consumption and, most importantly, in the ways that people formulate relationships; and 3) sarcasm and jaded narratives displace optimism about interracial relations and race prejudice in general.

ARCHIE BUNKER AS BIGOT (AND PROUD OF IT)

While most of the episodes of *All in the Family* dealt with race prejudice at least indirectly, and the 1971 episodes opened with a warning to that effect, eleven of them portray race prejudice directly. Most of these introduced the Black family, the Jeffersons, or dealt with Archie's associations with bigots (for example, "Lionel Moves into the Neighborhood," "Sammy's Visit," "Lionel Steps Out," and "Archie and the KKK"). Archie Bunker may be seen as a specimen of bigotry in the ways outlined by Ogles's proposal (1980) for developing observational concepts. According to Ogles, characteristics of Bunker's bigotry are 1) being impervious to criticism, 2) making direct derogatory remarks, 3) seeking redemption through his "defects" of character, and 4) establishing accommodating personal relationships with members of the African American race. After describing each of these features, this paper will identify the narrative structure used to create the Archie Bunker character.

Imperviousness to Criticism: In episode after episode, when Archie is criticized for his bigotry, he retains his closed mind. His son-in-law, Mike (called Meathead by Archie), often engages Archie in debate about race, only to have Archie reaffirm his position and values unchanged.

Mispronounced words and nonstandard grammar display Archie's lack of refinement and personal defensiveness which shield him from the onslaught of social change brought into his world by the likes of Mike, Lionel, and assorted characters who appear on the show. Archie's social network, on the other hand, consists of men who share his views and values. Even when Archie tries to withdraw from performing in a Black minstrel show that his lodge brothers are rehearsing, he does so, not so much from moral objection to "Black face" makeup, as from embarrassment. It is as if Archie wishes to retreat from engagement with his lodge brothers so as to isolate himself from counter pressures (his family's more liberal attitudes and the reactionary values of his lodge brothers).

Direct Derogatory Remarks: Archie racial remarks are unabashed. He seems to be unaware that his comments are directly negative, or implicitly derogatory. For example, he says, "Why should a spic object to being called a spic? That's what they are, ain't they?" Even when Mike or other characters on the show such as George Jefferson, the successful Black businessman next door to the Bunkers, confronts Archie, Archie acknowledges other views, but dismisses them.

Defects of Character: While Archie reflects a reactionary interpretation of the social changes that were playing themselves out in the aftermath of the Civil Rights movement and the Vietnam War, he seems to have a "heart." In episode after episode, he reveals his caring side. Archie is an unpolished gem, but a gem nonetheless. He seems like a victim, out of step with the tide of social change. If only he could see that his prejudiced views are self-defeating and at odds with social reality! Archie is redeemable as audiences later learned in his series, *Archie's Place*. The series, *Archie's Place*, however, "jumped the shark," since Archie, depicted there as a "recovering" bigot, diminished much of the interracial tension that made *All in the Family* magnetic.

Archie's defects were symbolic of the work that needed to be done in society to make racial equality a reality. He represents the hope that if defects can be identified and acknowledged, the dream of being judged by character and not skin color might still be a possibility.

Accommodating Personal Relationships: Archie tries to stop a Black family from moving into his neighborhood, only to discover that the family is Lionel's (Lionel was a friend of members of Archie's family). Archie finds himself involved in the details of the everyday lives of Lionel and his family. In doing so, Archie confronts the KKK and feels the tension between ties to his family and to his "values."

The viewer finds that Archie is not hopeless because he 1) has a support group that mirrors back to him the implications of his thinking and 2) he finds ways to live in an accommodative relationship with individual minority members whom he comes to know in everyday life situations.

Narrative Structure: The telling of the Bunker character is done primarily through conversational dialogue and personal appearance. Archie is clearly working class, and his speech is so laced with malapropisms that a new word came into the American vernacular: the Bunkerism (Rosa and Eschholz 1974). Examples of Archie's malapropos are:

> Nobody gets arrested in this country lest he deserves it. If he don't yell "pig" or any of them other epaulets, he'll be okay.
>
> Forget it. It's irrelevant. It ain't German to this conversation.
>
> Don't you never read the papers about all them unflocked priests running around? This here priest ain't kosher and never was.
>
> (About Mike) Listen to our world traveler, will ya? Ain't never been past the Chicago stock yards, and now he's a regular Marco Polish.

Larry David as Bigot (Trying Not to Be One)

The character of Larry David in *Curb Your Enthusiasm* is a device that displays a way of "producing and describing" society (Garfinkel and Rawls 2002, 66). Through Larry David's everyday life predicaments, the features of a postmodern society (Bauman 2000) are revealed. Hence, a detailed depiction of Davidisms as contrasted with Bunkerisms sheds light on the transformations of public discourse on race that have transpired over the three decades between the 1970s and the 2000s. During this period, racial injustice was vigorously attack in courts, educational institutions and on the interpersonal level with sometimes unanticipated results. This era was punctuated by progress and setbacks.

Klinkner and Smith (1999) argue that only under certain conditions is progress possible. These conditions are having to rely on the Black population during times of war, contradictions in the way Americans proclaim the value of equality and the way they act and international pressures to be consistent. Over the three decades from 1970 to 2000, these conditions waned with major setbacks, especially in the area of education (Kozol, 2005). Hence, a mixed and even paradoxical state of "equality" describes contemporary America.

The society of *Curb Your Enthusiasm* consists of a highly specialized and interrelated set of roles, e.g., restaurateurs, waiters, captains, chefs, masseurs, acupuncturists, lawyers, writers, agents, shopkeepers, sales people, therapists, psychics and a transmission specialist. Larry's inappropriate joke about the effects of affirmative action on the competency of a Black dermatologist damages subsequent relationships with Black people who show up in his life. And, Wanda, an assertive Black woman and Larry's wife's best friend, serves as a constant reminder to Larry of the struggles Blacks have in this life, in contrast to Larry's "white" and very successful way of life.

Various other characters appear in episodes and challenge Larry's assumptions about the meanings of race. For example, two such characters are Running Bear and the Korean caterer. Running Bear, a Native American gardener, whose magical healing powers conflict with middle-class notions of modesty revealed by Running Bear's matter of fact reference to Larry's wife's vagina, and Larry suspects the Korean caterer of using dog meat in a "special" carry-out dish he orders. Larry's assumptions are, of course, wrong but his warning about the possible dog meat to those attending a wedding reception results in mass nausea among the guests and casts Larry in the role of a bigot, again.

The Calculus of the Self: Larry negotiates identities and roles according to a calculus of self, particularly in his interracial affairs. In the episode, "Krazee-Eyez Killa," Larry is accused of betraying the confidences of his wife's best friend, Wanda, who is engaged to Krazee-Eyez, a rapper. While Larry and Cheryl, his wife, are attending an engagement party for Wanda and Krazee-Eyez Killa, Larry is obviously uncomfortable at the party (he amuses himself by popping the bubbles of packing material). At Cheryl's insistence, he stays at the party instead of leaving and is drawn into a conversation with Krazee-Eyez who seeks Larry advice about a lyric he is working on. Larry unintentionally befriends Killa by suggesting changes to the lyrics (Larry suggests that Killa has one too many "mudder fuckers" in them). Later, Larry alienates Jeff's wife Susie by passing up her house-tour offer, then runs into problems trying to replace a sports jacket Cheryl threw out.

Larry's problem is to replace the jacket that he took, against wardrobe rules. He needs it for a retake of a scene from a movie in which he is playing a gangster. He finds the identical jacket in Krazee-Eyez Killa's closet during a house tour that he agreed to on the occasion of a "pop in" at Killa's house. Larry learned to appreciate the importance of a house tour from his earlier refusal of Susie's invitation, since Susie called Larry a "freak of fuckin' nature" for refusing a house tour.

At each juncture in this clever narrative, Larry uses those around him to achieve his ends. In the end, of course, Larry loses Killa's respect (Larry is no longer Killa's "Caucasian"), the jacket he needed, and Wanda's confidence, which he never really had. Saved by a back-up jacket, which the wardrobe master keeps, Larry's instrumental attitude serves as the background for humor in the scene as he chokes on a pubic hair stuck in his throat from oral sex with his wife (oral sex having been the subject of a bond in the party conversation between Killa and Larry).

Mutual Instrumentalism: Clearly, the friendship between Killa and Larry is based on mutual instrumentality. For Larry, it was the good fortune of Killa's having a sports jacket that he needs, and for Killa, it was having an accomplished comedy writer as a friend. Killa remains intimidating and potentially dangerous, while Larry is hapless and victimized, trying to look like he can handle the racial issue. Race roles are inverted, and Larry struggles to extricate himself from reciprocal obligations to Killa.

Larry's action is, of course, a marked contrast to Archie's increasing and enduring involvement in the lives of the Jeffersons. Archie protests his interaction with the Jeffersons but becomes deeply involved in an interracial relationship with them. Larry David establishes racial relationships quickly, but they are revealed as shallow and short-lived. These two features of Larry David's character (calculus of the self and mutual instrumentalism) take on particular significance when placed in the context of postmodernity.

Postmodern Sensibilities: The most obvious features of postmodern style embodied in the Larry David character are parody, pastiche, playfulness, the pseudo-event, recursiveness, and irony (Bauman 2000, Elias 1982, Grossberg 1992).

Selected lexicon, dialogue, and context illustrate the pervasiveness of these sensibilities in the world of *Curb Your Enthusiasm*. Parody, of course, imitates and reinterprets social phenomena as satire. *Curb Your Enthusiasm* is a parody. It is both a light-hearted and a deep look at the meaning of everyday life, friendships, commitments, caring, troubles, and life itself. Larry comments that he feels compelled to say "hi" to Black strangers. However, he interacts uncomfortably with Blacks, as in his faux pas by telling the racist joke in the company of Blacks in the episode, "Affirmative Action," and as in his being verbally harassed for being a racist by an African American actress Larry rejected during a casting for television program he was producing.

Whereas parody produces satire, pastiche imitates life. In "Trick or Treat," Larry and Cheryl attend the premiere of a movie written by his disabled friend, Cliff Cobb, during which Larry manages to offend a Jewish neighbor by whistling (imitating) Wagner tunes (Wagner was anti-Semitic) while waiting in line for the show. In another episode ("The Bracelet"), when Larry fails to purchase a bracelet for his wife on her birthday, he makes amends with the perfect gift of a romantic morning: live chamber music (Wagner again) on their lawn to serenade Cheryl. In still another episode ("Mary, Joseph and Larry"), Larry suggests his Hispanic gardener use the familiar "tu" form of Spanish pronouns with him, while giving his gardener a Christmas tip, not realizing that the "tu" form should emanate from the gardener, himself. The audience is prompted to feel the agony of embarrassment for Larry's ill-formed attempts at social graces.

Larry's imitations of Wagner's music, of celebrity voices and tones, of romantic interludes, of a gangster in a Martin Scorsese film, and the use of "tu" with his gardener are all examples of pastiche. Larry's imitations are overtly staged as in his grandiose sing-song apology: "N-E-S-T-L-E-S, Nestles makes the very best, SORRY!" Self-awareness of action is communicated through absurd juxtapositions and through exaggeration.

The comedic quality of *Curb Your Enthusiasm* is further enhanced, similarly to *Seinfeld*, by the musical score that runs throughout the series. Flute notes fluttering over the lugubrious sousaphone line frame as buffoon-like Larry's having his front teeth knocked out by Ted Danson's kid, or his imitation of a coffee commercial. Obviously, the concept for the series is a stream of pseudo-events, that is, running portrayals of everyday life scenes.

Another comedic device abounding in *Curb Your Enthusiasm* is irony. From a "David Promise" to elevator etiquette, Larry says and does one thing and means exactly the opposite. Larry's "borrowing" a restaurant fork to help a "working man, the limousine driver" results in his receiving a Scarlet Letter Punishment (walking in front of the restaurant wearing a sandwich sign reading "I STEAL FORKS FROM RESTAURANTS!").

In the episode "Affirmative Action," Larry insults a Black physician by remarking to his friend Richard in the presence of the physician, "You let this guy treat you, even with affirmative action?" Then, Larry accounts for his gaffe in terms of his being overly affable. Being overly affable results in insults to Blacks; being too caring to the working man results in Larry's public punishment.

Larry's apologies often become affronts because of the way he persists in his definitions of the situation. Larry's denial of discrimination against Black actors when a Black female actor, whom he rejected for a casting, confronts him becomes "evidence" of his racism to her, and Larry responds with a string of apologies. Throughout the episodes, Larry's good intentions turn bad, his altruism becomes self-serving, and his argumentative playfulness produces serious affronts and insults.

He often jokes about racial stereotypes, as though the person of another race or culture is "wise enough" to handle the joke, without questioning the racialized meanings that underlie the joke. For example, when he tries to explain the joke about affirmative action to the dermatologist in terms his being overly affable, the doctor is clearly incensed.

The character of Larry David frames race as a category, a way of talking that neither solves problems nor offers hope that the prejudice gap can ever be closed. In the closing scenes of "Affirmative Action," Larry ends up in front a group of professional Black folks who are visiting at the Black physician's home. Congenially and in a forgiving spirit, they request that Larry explain the ill-fated joke that started all the trouble. Of course, retelling the joke simply makes matters worse, and finally, the woman Larry rejected for a part appears and rants on about Larry's being a racist, heaping on more of the public scolding he gets for several unintended gaffes.

Larry insists that he has a "special relationship" with Blacks and other minorities, as in his off again, on again relations with the Lesbian community. His special relationship with Wanda, a Black woman who is Larry's wife's best friend, is often problematic. For example, Wanda berates Larry for assuming that a passing Black pedestrian in a parking lot intends to steal his car. However, when Larry shepherds Wanda's manuscript for a potential television series through the review process, the tables are turned. Larry has to tell Wanda that her writing was rejected. She replies, "Did you tell them I'm Black?" and then proceeds to berate Larry about how he should have played the "race card" on behalf of her manuscript review.

Larry's relationships with minorities are conflicted and ironic, as in gaining, then losing his identity as Krazie-Eyed Killa's "Caucasian." And, in another episode, Larry persists in calling an interracial doll a "mulatto doll," after being corrected by several Blacks and whites in the know. Over and over, Larry's acts of caring are tinged by his superficial assumptions about the nature of equality and social justice.

Narrative Devices in Curb Your Enthusiasm

Larry's character is developed through situationally appropriate uses of lexicon, that is, the style of interaction and the presentational forms are driven by a kind of talk about talk. Some of these phases, the contexts in which they are used, and the things they are intended to accomplish pertaining to race or ethnic identity are listed below and provide material for comparison of Davidisms with Bunkerisms. Here are two examples:

> Are you my Caucasian? What Larry affectionately asks Krazee-Eyez.
>
> Jews with Trees: Larry, vehemently opposes Jews having Christmas trees in their homes, says, "There's nothing worse than Jews with trees."

From Bigotry to Sarcasm

In *All in the Family*, Archie Bunker's scripts are replete with bigoted malaproprisms, simultaneously illustrating Archie's ignorance and stubbornness. Archie thinks of himself as knowledgeable and well-informed, but his non-standard grammar and malaproprisms expose the weakness of his opinions. What he says, especially about race, is discredited by the way he says it. And, since the audience "gets it," the content of his remarks often go unchallenged. To the extent that the nature of bigotry is addressed, it is through the predicaments that Archie creates for himself. Archie's character evokes in the audience an initial repulsion, followed by pity, then eventually sympathy from the audience, triggering a cycle of redemption through which conventional or "proper" norms of equality are established. That is, standard values of integration, equal rights and participation in society are reinforced while Archie blunders his way through social change as a relic of a changing past.

In contrast, for Larry David in *Curb Your Enthusiasm*, bigoted blunders emerge from simply doing everyday life. When race is introduced into Larry's world, he is not a bigot and he is far from incompetent or ignorant. Nonetheless, the predicaments of his everyday life set him apart from the notion that race fades into norms of inclusion. In the world according to Larry David, his self-conscious engagement with racialized others sharply defines his identity. Larry knows just enough about diversity to be like the average "good American" who does not have close relationships with people of different races, but who cares to think of himself as a person without prejudice.

Larry cares about race. But because Larry's knowledge and sensitivity to cultural nuances is postmodern, he often botches his opportunities to bond and has to do considerable remedial work because of his gaffes. Larry even refers to himself as the master of supplication. He devotes much of his everyday existence to shoring up fractured relationships through apologies and feigned contrition. These are presented to others in such a way that they show his frustration with having revealed his flaw, a flaw that is often only in the eye of the other. In Krazee-Eyez Killa, Larry goes from being trusted brother ("you my Caucasian") to ordinary, distance Caucasian (his friendship with Killa ending when Killa demands the return of his jacket and confronts Larry about it in his home).

What the viewer receives from the Larry David character is a resignation made palatable through an interpretation framed by experiences in a postmodern society. That is, despite a self-defined, non-bigoted Jewish guy's best attempts, race seems to be here to stay. It becomes a topic for humor by virtue of how it is talked about. The way Larry, his wife (who, like Archie's wife Edith, seems to bear no prejudice), and the racial characters talk about race reflects how bigotry in white society continues and how those of other races cope with it.

In *Curb Your Enthusiasm*, interracial relationships end in problematic ways. White comedian Richard Lewis's courtship with a Black woman, for example, ends because of Richard's anxiety about the truth of the belief that Black men have large penises. Richard was afraid to have sex with his girlfriend, fearing embarrassment by way of comparison with Black men she may have known. In the aftermath of such situations, we are left with talk itself as a means of showing a resigned acknowledgment of the current state of interracial attitudes.

CONCLUSIONS

Comparing the narratives of race in *All in the Family* and *Curb Your Enthusiasm* depicts the shifts that have occurred in the everyday experiences of race in America over a 30-year period. While turbulent and conflicted, the 1970s offered an optimistic and assimilative vision for our culture regarding race and race prejudice. In the redeeming of Archie Bunker and the establishment of everyday interactive networks that cut across stereotypical understandings of race, a hopeful model of a new social order was presented. It was a model of a racially integrated society where race distinctions fade into mundane problems.

With Larry David, the meanings of race assume a postmodern sensibility, which means, among other things, that race becomes a category of meaning in everyday life, situated and negotiable—a part of the way things are. Race becomes a mundane problem. Conceptions of race have shifted from fixed, definitional, and "individualized" contents towards contents which are more situational, fluid, and ironic. This shift parallels societal transformations from modern to postmodern. And finally, *Curb Your Enthusiasm*'s sarcastic narratives of the consequences of interracial relations and race prejudice have displaced optimistic and challenging portrayals. For their respective eras, each program reflects conceptions of race in popular consciousness.

NOTE

1. Parts of this chapter were previously published in *Studies in Symbolic Interaction* 32 (2008): 183–198.

Chapter Five

Laughter and Humor in the Classroom and Beyond

My students used to tell me that I was funny—in a Woody Allen kind of way.[1] I took that as a compliment and just kept on teaching in my own way throughout my career. I became familiar with some literature on humor, but not until I retired did I start to think more about the role that laughter and humor play in our everyday lives, and how the intersections of identities such as class, race, ethnicity, and age become fodder for what Murray Davis called the "humanizer."

A few years after my retirement, I discovered that I missed teaching and I went back to work at a local university, but I struggled to find ways to connect with students whose life experiences bore little resemblance to mine. I used Tim Delaney's *Seinology* (2006) as a way to enliven introduction to sociology, and I even conducted a workshop called "Seinfeld in Sociology: Using Popular Culture to Explore Course Concepts."[2]

I discovered that Jerry Seinfeld's humor more often than not missed the mark with 19- to 23-year-olds. However, more mature students laughed at the episodes that exposed awkward moments of everyday life and the playful portrayals of the meanings of social categories. Not only did the younger students not get the jokes, they failed see how the themes of the episodes connected with sociological concepts. Much to my chagrin, I questioned how much I really knew about what makes people laugh and what is considered funny. Shortly after this, I retired again.

A few years later, the urge to teach returned. This time I taught in a program for elderly, retired folks. Many were professionals, people engaged in business, and a few retired professors. Typical courses offered through this program included topics of local interest, music, foreign affairs, evolution or some other contemporary aspect of science, health, medical technology, crafts, yoga, and Tai Chi. I wondered if sociology would interest the curriculum committee responsible for choosing classes and, then, if sociology would attract a respectable crowd? When searching for a class to teach, I combined my curiosity about why my young university students failed to appreciate Seinfeld with my desire to profess sociology. I decided that a course on humor would be a way to allow me to research an interesting topic and practice furtive sociology along the way.

The program, called Life Quest, offers eight-week sessions for senior adults with class meetings once a week for 50 minutes. My challenge was to find ways to infuse sociology into my discussion about the nature of laughter and humor. A paper I delivered at a sociology convention, "Contented People are Not Funny," launched me into the sociological literature on humor, and, as I mentioned, I had been told over the years that I was occasionally funny in the classroom. I taught three classes of about 25 white seniors, an equal mix of men and women, most of them with upper middle-class incomes and college education, some with professional degrees. Over a two-year period, I taught classes called, respectively, "Why We Laugh: The Social Dimensions of Humor," "More Laughter," and "Still Laughing."

This paper is about teaching, with a smile or even a laugh. It recommends an approach to teaching sociology based on internet technology (YouTube) and the use of scholarly literature on laughing and humor to introduce sociology to students who might not otherwise be attracted to the discipline. I suggest that the study of humor may be used as a furtive approach to teaching sociology. While the class I present here was developed for an elderly, mostly retired professional audience, portions of the materials suggested may be used in college level introductory and even in some upper-level courses. I cobbled this approach together through life experiences which I share in this article. While using humor as a pedagogical device to illustrate concepts and even theories is not new, the approach I suggest is possible only because of the development of YouTube as an archive of clips of comedians, television sit-coms and even enactments of historic comedic performances.

WHAT'S BEEN DONE

Others have used humor to teach sociology, but none with the benefit of access to video clips of comedians via YouTube. Pre-YouTube, Hynes (1989) relates how he used ethnographic descriptions of Western Apaches to explain why Apaches think a joke about "white men" is funny. By identifying violations of their cultural rules, he illustrated sociological principles. For example, he illustrated that Apaches value the group and American students, the individual, using Durkheim's types of solidarity, and Goffman's concept of the presentation of self. Bingham and Hernandez (2009) pointed out the similarities between the comedic eye and the sociological imagination as a rationale for incorporating comedy into their class presentations. They rely on sociological analysis to legitimate the use of a wide variety of comedic materials from George Carlin, *The Daily Show*, to satirical articles from magazines. Bingham and Hernandez provided an impressive table of comedic sources, then offered some survey evidence showing the effectiveness of these materials with undergraduate students. My use of YouTube clips and contemporary literature and research extends applications of humor and provides a furtive introduction to sociology.

My students had an average age of early 70s. As I mentioned, most of them were college educated, but their employment histories were varied and the subject of sociology was foreign, or a vague memory, to them. I was intent on avoiding what Bingham and Hernandez characterize as the "doom and gloom" of scholarly analysis. My goal was to introduce the sociological imagination and hope that these students might appreciate it. Above all, however, I wanted to keep it funny! I tried to remember Mark Twain's wisdom: "Explaining humor is a lot like dissecting a frog: you learn a lot in the process, but in the end, you kill it."

A Note about Method

Over the last decade the scope and sophistication of YouTube has grown so that it is possible to mine YouTube for just about any topic you can think of. Especially, for comedy, YouTube has become a treasure trove. Using very simple key word searches, I was able to locate clips that illustrated virtually all the points I had made on my PowerPoint presentation. After I found an appropriate clip, I used Ummy Video Downloader to save the clips to my computer, and from there, I inserted them into PowerPoint.

This method of mining YouTube has been particularly effective for avoiding "killing the frog," since the clips are sure to elicit a laugh, a chuckle, or at least a groan.

The Biology of Laughter

Some goals of the class were to review the scholarly and popular literature on humor and to establish an understanding of the difference between laughter and humor. The latter is essentially social in nature and the former, biological.

Table 5.1.   YouTube Clips by Categories

Categories of Humor	YouTube Clips
Biology of Laughter and Humor	Clip One: Laughing Rats https://www.youtube.com/watch?v=d-84UJpYFRM; Clip Two: Koko and Willams https://www.youtube.com/watch?v=GorgFtCqPEs.
Explanations	Clip Three: Schadenfreude MP3; Clip Four: Obama on Trump https://www.youtube.com/watch?v=k8TwRmX6zs4; Clip Five: Dick Van Dyke https://www.youtube.com/watch?v=sRaF4gk1yhY; Cllip Six: Bill Irvin https://www.youtube.com/watch?v=EDIQp5pbAl8.
Social and Cultural Attacks	Clip Seven: Dennis Miller https://www.youtube.com/watch?v=Gtnu9b701RE; Clip Eight: https://www.youtube.com/watch?v=tptLry5pc4g; Clip Nine: George Carlin https://www.youtube.com/watch?v=wUG0IMjfxCE .
Gender (in order of stages)	Clip Ten: Gracie tells a story https://www.youtube.com/watch?v=AlFCKZkeBrg; Clip Eleven: Candy Factory https://www.youtube.com/watch?v=WmAwcMNxGqM; Clip Twelve: Carol Burnett https://www.youtube.com/watch?v=FqPVfHnd3nk; Clip Fifteen: Phyllis Diller https://www.youtube.com/watch?v=Zl3fRnmEKgM; Clip Sixteen: Joan Rivers https://www.youtube.com/watch?v=oWnclpPuNJo; Clip Eighteen: Ellen Degeneres https://www.youtube.com/watch?v=YlAAl3j_vsY; Clip Nineteen: Amy Schumer https://www.youtube.com/watch?v=zhu7rs3lhas.
Alienation	Clip Sixteen: Woody Allen https://www.youtube.com/watch?v=_elqqiEYOAs; Clip Seventeen: David and Lewis https://www.youtube.com/watch?v=uQbnjo3vxrw; Clip Eighteen: Wanda Sykes https://www.youtube.com/watch?v=KGYzKkhtumg.
Race	Clip Nineteen: Chitlin Circuit https://www.youtube.com/watch?v=Pyw8NxlURnc; Clip Twenty: Amos and Andy https://www.youtube.com/watch?v=griMGY-JLvo; Clip Twenty Two: Apollo Theater https://www.youtube.com/watch?v=zVnYsgDjQ_8; Clip Twenty Three: Bill Cosby https://www.youtube.com/watch?v=bputeFGXEjA; Clip Twenty Four: David Chappelle https://www.youtube.com/watch?v=JJ3dk6KAvQM.
More Tension	Clip Twenty-Five: Michael Jr. https://www.youtube.com/watch?v=LbP4KttZOcc; Clip Twenty: Six: Blue-Collar Jokes https://www.youtube.com/watch?v=ZqHPqTDHxJs; Clip Twenty Seven: Josh Blue https://www.youtube.com/watch?v=Nhuq1Hz22UA; Clip Twenty Eight: Chris Gethard https://www.youtube.com/watch?v=HWf1hME-GxQ.
Sarcasm	Clip Twenty-Nine: Jerry Seinfeld https://www.youtube.com/watch?v=xR1ckgXN8G0.

Since the scope and volume of the literature is overwhelming, I decided to discuss examples of various approaches. For the sociological understanding, I referred to Berger (2014) and Davis (1993). For the philosophical, I used Critchley (2002); for the psychological, Martin (2007), and for the popular, I chose McGraw and Warner (2014).

Following the classic symbolic interactionists, I began my presentation with current knowledge of the biological nature of the phenomena being examined. For example, W. I. Thomas posited four wishes that were said to be grounded in the biology of the person (Colyer 2015). Also, G. H. Mead (1934) suggested that the developmental emergence of the self was predicated on the innate capabilities of the organism (see his discussion of the "I" in *Mind, Self and Society* 1934, 203–204).

I started with the biology of laughter as a physiological response to stimulation consisting of two parts: a set of gestures and the production of a sound. When we laugh, both of those activities occur simultaneously. Many parts of our bodies (arms, legs, and trunk muscles) can be involved. Brain (2017) states that when we laugh fifteen facial muscles contract and stimulate the zygomatic major muscle (the upper lip), and our respiratory system is upset by the epiglottis half-closing the larynx, so that air intake occurs irregularly. Tear ducts may activate and the opening and closing of the mouth restricts oxygen intake. Faces become moist and often red (or purple), and, noises that laughter makes range from sedate giggles to boisterous guffaws. In short, we nearly suffocate when we laugh.

A scientific specialty called gelotology (Brain 2017) tells us how the brain is involved in laughter. It seems that the left side of the cortex (the layer of cells that covers the entire surface of the forebrain) analyzes the words and structure of a joke or a social situation, while the frontal lobe, which is involved in social emotional responses, becomes very active. In the case of a joke, the right hemisphere of the cortex carries out the intellectual analysis required to "get" the joke. Brainwave activity then spreads to the sensory processing area of the occipital lobe (the area on the back of the head that contains the cells that process visual signals). The limbic system also is involved in laughter, as it is with motivation and emotion. The amygdala and hippocampus, as well as the medial dorsal nucleus of the thalamus, are active in friendship, love, and affection, and in the expression of mood. And, the hypothalamus, particularly its median part, has been identified as a major center in the production of loud, uncontrollable laughter.

To carry out this biological approach, I turned to the evolutionary psychology (Martin 2007) that offers several plausible explanations for the emergence of laughter and humor. Laughter, so the theory goes, may have begun as a gesture of shared relief at the passing of danger. And, since the relaxation that results from a bout of laughter inhibits the biological fight-or-flight response, laughter may indicate trust in one's companions. It seems reasonable, therefore, to conclude that the purpose of laughter is likely related to making and strengthening social connections. Laughter occurs when people are comfortable with one another. The more laughter, the more bonding within the group. This feedback loop of bonding-laughter-more bonding, combined with the common desire not to be singled out from the group, may be another reason why laughter is often contagious.

Laughter in a group has a social control function as well. Through laughter the emotional climate of the group may be controlled. Hence, laughter must have evolved to change the behavior of others. For example, in an embarrassing or threatening situation, laughter may serve as a conciliatory gesture or as a way to deflect anger. If the threatening person joins the laughter, the risk of confrontation lessens. Laughter functions as a kind of social signal. For example, subjects in an experiment were 30 times more likely to laugh in social settings than when alone (and without pseudo-social stimuli like television). Even nitrous oxide, or laughing gas, loses much of its oomph when taken in solitude (Brain 2017). This observation provides an opportunity to discuss the power of social influences as reported in Becker's oft quoted "Becoming a Marihuana User" (Becker 1953).

At this point in the class, I introduce the perennial question about how distinctive human beings are from other animals (Irvine 2004, 2017). It seems the curve of research evidence is toward a blurred line between species. I show a YouTube clip about rats laughing when tickled by researchers (Clip One, Table 5.1) and another about visits that the late comedian Robin Williams made to Koko the signing gorilla (Clip Two, Table 5.1), in which each makes the other laugh.

This section of the class suggests that laughter is probably distinctively human, at least in its frequency and functionality; that laughter is complex physically and neurologically, and it functions primarily to increase social bonding. The class was amused by giggling rats and moved by the emotional connection between a man and a great ape.

The Social Nature of Humor

Much of what we laugh at is not funny; for instance, nervous or taunting laughter. So what is humor? Could it be a social construction built on the biology of laughter? Explanations of humor have been offered by canonical philosophers such as Kant, Schopenhauer, Hobbs, and others. Critchley (2002) offers a pithy and contemporary overview of the explanations of these thinkers and their philosophical context. Not surprisingly, extant explanations of humor stress that cognition plays an essential role. For example, incongruity theory suggests that humor arises when logic and familiarity are replaced by things that do not normally go together. A joke becomes funny when we expect one outcome and another happens. When a joke begins, our minds and bodies are already anticipating what's going to happen. That anticipation takes the form of logical thought intertwined with emotion and is influenced by our past experiences and our thought processes. Critchley (2002, 39 and 85) traces this explanation to Kant.

Another account claims social hierarchy is involved. According to superiority theory, we laugh at jokes that focus on someone else's mistakes, stupidity, or misfortune. We feel superior to this person, experience a certain detachment from the situation, and so we are able to laugh at it, *schadenfreude*. At this juncture in my PowerPoint, I have embedded an mp3 file of the song "Schadenfreude" from the musical, *Avenue Q* (Clip Three, Table 5.1). I play that clip and then one of President Barack Obama's comments at the National Press Association dinner in which he lampoons Donald Trump about the President's place of birth. Some political pundits claim this so enraged Trump that he was furthered motivated to run for the office: a powerful man using humor to establish superiority over a critic. As Critchley suggests, this theory was anticipated by Hobbs (Clip Four, Table 5.1).

Relief theory points to the use of devices (stories, movements, sounds, or sights) that build tension of suspense. Then the tension is broken down with a side comment, enabling the viewer to relieve pent-up emotion. When coping with two sets of emotions and thoughts, people may need release and laughter as a way of relieving their system of the tension of incongruity. Hence, dark or gallows humor can function as a coping mechanism for those in stressful situations.

A recent social psychological attempt to explain humor comes from Peter McGraw's benign-violation theory. Extrapolating from Thomas Veatch's model, McGraw suggests that humor occurs in the overlap between violation of a norm, rule, or some aspect of everyday life and the nature of the violation, that is, it benign or egregious.

McGraw has tested many aspects of the theory, published scholarly articles and a book (*The Humor Code*, with Joel Warner). Humor occurs when and only when three conditions are satisfied: 1) a situation is perceived as a violation, 2) the situation is also perceived as benign, and 3) both perceptions occur simultaneously. For example, play fighting and tickling, which produce laughter in humans (and other primates), are benign violations because they are physically threatening but are emotionally and physically harmless attacks.

A violation refers to anything that threatens one's beliefs about how the world should be. From an evolutionary perspective, humorous violations likely originated as threats to physical well-being (e.g., the attacks that make up tickling and play fighting), but expanded to include threats to psychological well-being (e.g., insults, sarcasm), including behaviors that break social norms (e.g., strange behaviors, flatulence), cultural norms (e.g., unusual accents, most scenes from the movie *Borat*), linguistic norms (e.g., puns, malapropisms), logic norms (e.g., absurdities, nonsequiturs), and moral norms (e.g., disrespectful behavior, bestiality)

A situation is not funny when it depicts a violation that does not simultaneously seem benign, or when it depicts a benign situation that has no violation. For example, play fighting and tickling cease to elicit laughter either when the attack stops (strictly benign) or becomes too aggressive (a malign violation). Jokes similarly fail to be funny when either they are too tame or too risqué or in poor taste. For example, "Look, up in the sky, it's a bird, it's a plane. I don't know what it is but it's heading to the Twin Towers."

For a violation to produce humor, it also needs to be perceived as benign. McGraw's research suggests three ways that a violation can seem benign: 1) alternative norms (e.g., one meaning of a phrase in a pun doesn't make sense, but the other meaning does), 2) commitment to a violated norm (e.g., men find sexist jokes funnier than women do), and 3) psychological distance (e.g., "comedy is tragedy plus time").

Having reviewed and illustrated the state of the science about humor, I introduce the idea that some forms of laughter and humor are universal, and this provides an opening to discuss the attempts by twentieth century sociologists and anthropologists to uncover social and cultural universals. Slapstick and visual humor appear to be present in all cultures. This probably is because the antics of a humorist seem to be physical pain or injury (violation), but are not (benign). I show first a clip from *The Dick Van Dyke Show* in which Van Dye performs a routine from his earlier comedy career in which he "hurts" himself in a variety of ways, and then a clip of Bill Irwin, an actor and trained clown performing with his body, including a disappearing walk into a footlocker (Clips Five and Six, Table 5.1).

What's So Funny

By now, the class is laughing and looking forward to the next session during which they will receive a full dose of sociology, although I never use the "s" word. It begins with Berger (2014) who reminds us of Dionysus, the Greek god who violates all ordinary boundaries, as do his devotees. Comedy, Berger suggests, retains Dionysian features, even if in modernity it is toned down or even defanged (Berger 2014, 24). The two features of comedy dangerous to all established order are: 1) the cognitive skill of "standing outside" the fundamentals of everyday life and, 2) joining together what convention and morality keep apart. Here are examples of the destructive nature of laughter: *Omuneepo* (the Tanzanian laughing disease); kids getting tickled in church or school, the class clown, and a personal example from a fellow chorus singer and I when we experienced uncontrollable laughter while singing the background for the Billy Joel's "The Longest Time" ("'bung oo ah oo ah"). We were asked by the chorus director to please leave the rehearsal to compose ourselves as adults (I was 68 years of age at the time).

> [Comedy] must be contained . . . ritualized into socially acceptable forms and confined within the boundaries of the dramatic stage. The spectators laugh in the theater, and that may keep them from laughing in and laughing at the solemn performances of religion and the state. (Berger, 2014, 26)

With this introduction, I present the seminal work of Murray Davis (1993) whose *What's So Funny: The Comic Conception of Culture and Society* is a standard for sociological analysis on humor. His contention, consistent with Berger's, is that humor is an attack on culture and society, that is, it is a form of resistance against the mechanisms of social control.

According to Davis, comedy attacks culture with incongruity and ambiguity. People organize and manage their beliefs and values. They use what they know about the social world to make sense out of what they hear in an interactive exchange. Categorical thinking and perhaps, most importantly, the way people hear meanings (Sacks 1974), describes how people understand and accomplish conversations. Systems of knowledge and feelings, or at the very least, routine and habituated practices, are implicit in humor.

Humor exploits the assumptions of everyday life. Davis's book is full of jokes and stories that illustrate each of the tactics that humor employs to attack culture and society. For example, puns and word play exploit the unstable meanings of cultural categories of knowledge, what Davis calls "irrational logic" (juxtaposing two or more terms whose relationship is irrational). He cites from a joke book he inherited from his father to illustrate his points: two drunks walking down a railroad track. One complains, "Damn, this is a long flight of steps." The other counters, "I don't mind the steps so much, it's the low railings that get me."

Inauthentic presentation is another tool for irrational logic. It works by revealing the disparity between knowing and being, logic and life. This is often done through exposing the spectrum of humanity from super to subhuman. "Two kangaroos are talking to each other, and one says to the other, 'Gee, I hope it doesn't rain today. I hate it when the children have to play inside.'"

I use these jokes to discuss the nature of cultural knowledge, following Spradley (Nash and McCurdy 1990) and cognitive science (Lakoff and Johnson 1980). I emphasize the agency of actors and Swidler's (1986) "tool bag" analogy. Humor may be often overlooked as a powerful tool for resisting and manipulating culture.

Davis's theory of humor also extends to attacks on society. He refers to wit's weapons, among which is making fun of people or shifting from one social unit to another to create tension for humor. He identifies atypical actors, atypical action, incompletely functioning (I have a twin brother, he's not too smart. Last year he forgot my birthday), inauthentic presentation or self-deprecation (When I was a kid, I was so weak that I got beaten up by my imaginary friends), and incomparable selves (tension from within as in "Loaned a friend money for plastic surgery. Now I can't recognize him to collect my money").

Humor is one tool in the tool kit that people acquire through the socialization process. They can use humor to attack culture and society, that is, to deal with constraints and forces beyond their control. Humor is a form of talking that has an identifiable organization, devices for its production, and practical accomplishments. Different expressions of humor accomplish different results in social interaction. I illustrate with clips of Dennis Miller dismissing global warming, John Fugelsang depicting God as an alcoholic father, and George Carlin's rant on everyday language expressions (Clips Seven, Eight, and Nine, Table 5.1).

Gender and Comedy

Sociology tells coherent and well-documented stories about how the lives of people, in a given society, vary according to gender, age, class and status, race and ethnicity, and interactions among these aspects, for example (gender interacting with age race, and so on). I follow this rather audacious declaration with a discussion of the General Social Survey and announce that of these categories, race is the most significant for most attitudes and measures of location in society.

Then, I proceed to discuss comedy as shaped by each social category. First, gender. As far back as we have records, men have dominated comedy. Women, of course, use humor, but not in a formal role until the late nineteenth and twentieth centuries. One recalls Sarah's reaction to Abraham's chat with God: Sarah laughed to herself, saying, "After I have become old, shall I have pleasure, my lord being old also?"

Women played active roles in vaudeville, mostly performing musical comedy in couple acts. And, there was the Elinore Sisters in the early 1920s doing a straight man and funny man act, and cracking Irish and other ethnic jokes.

The post-vaudeville period cast women in comedic roles in the movies, especially during and shortly after WWII. Then radio adopted headlines from the dying stage of vaudeville. Almost exclusively men, these comedians established themselves as true celebrities (Jack Benny, Bob Hope, and a host of others). Among them was one woman: Judy Canova, who pioneered in sketch comedy. Other women began to try their hand at comedy with great success. Among these early highly successful comedians were Lucille Ball, and later, Carol Burnett. To illustrate the typical materials and styles of women in comedy, I play Clip Ten, Table 5.1 (Burns and Allen doing a vaudeville routine on their TV show circa 1957) and Clip Eleven (Lucy's candy factory sketch) and Clip Twelve (Carol Burnett's exercise routine).

Women moved from sketch and narrative comedy to standup. The two breakthrough acts were Phyllis Diller and Joan Rivers (Clips Thirteen and Fourteen, Table 5.1). They employed the same style as men but the content of their routines was distinctively shaped by the sex roles of the period. Comedic themes in women's humor from the 1900s to the 1960s created comedic tension through playing on domestic roles, using physical humor and attacking social roles. These women were competing with men for appearances on TV and time on the stages of Las Vegas. This juncture in the class is apropos to discuss how changing demographics and modernization itself alter sex roles and lead to changes in the meanings and language of gender. I refer to Guttentag and Secord (1983) and their sex ratio hypothesis. Then, I review current literature on gender inequality. I conclude this week's class with YouTube clips of two women comedians I suggest represent contemporary trends: Ellen DeGeneres (circa 1985) and a 2017 hosting of *Saturday Night Liveies* by Amy Schumer (Clips Fifteen and Sixteen, Table 5.1).

I summarize gender and comedy by discussing women in comedy in the larger context of the waves of feminism in the United States. The first wave (1830s to early 1900s) involved the struggle for rights to enter contracts, own property, and vote. The second (1950s to 1980s) focused on workplace equality, changes in the family and sexuality, including reproductive rights and the passage of the Equal Rights Amendment.

The Third Wave of feminism (1980s to present) deals with the micro-politics of gender equality. Today's issues derive from previous waves of feminism, such as disparities in male and female pay, the reproductive rights of women, and ending violence against women in our nation as well as that of others. We discuss how the term "feminist" is more widely accepted, yet diverse in its meanings. There are the ego-cultural feminists, radicals, liberal/reformers, electoral, academic, ecofeminists, and others. The issues are in the details of everyday life, and feminism is best understood as the theory of the political, economic, and social equality of the sexes. I suggest that we can group the comedians now according to waves: The first wave includes vaudeville: Judy Canova, Lucille Ball, Gracie Allen, and the second: Phyllis Diller and Joan Rivers. The third closes with a diverse collection of sketches from Amy Schumer, Rachel Feinstein, and Sarah Silverman.

Comedy and Alienation

A distinctively modern form of tension, so the literature suggests (Haiman 1998) is alienation. Of course, separation from others and even oneself is a constant theme of Western civilization, but it seems that various forms of alienation are associated with the modernization process. While this topic is vast, I found a simple way to tie alienation and humor together. I used Seeman's (1959) survey of how the term was used in sociological research. He identified five operationalized meanings of the term: powerlessness, estrangement, isolation, meaninglessness, and anomie. My intent here is to link each meaning to humor.

Powerlessness: a New Yorker cartoon of two haggard, emaciated, lice-ridden men, shackled hands and feet to a wall in a dungeon. Far above them there is a small window with iron bars. One man turns to the other and says, "Now, listen—here's my plan" (*New Yorker*, Shel Silverstein).

Estrangement: another cartoon of two women at a juice bar discussing their relationships with men. One says to the other: "Sex brought us together—gender drove us apart" (*New Yorker*). *Meaninglessness:* "Sex without love is a meaningless experience, but as meaningless experiences go its pretty damned good" (Woody Allen, Clip Seventeen, Table 5.1). *Isolation:* a mantra for meditation (*Curb Your Enthusiasm*, Clip Eighteen, Table 5.1), and "I'm alone in a car pool" (Richard Lewis). *Normlessness or anomie:* "Went to a reform Temple. Started to pray and the congregation started a wave" (Richard Lewis) and Clip Nineteen (Table 5.1) of Wanda Sykes being interviewed on the *Ellen DeGeneres* show about living in a home with a white wife and two white children, feeling like the help.

African Americans

In this session of the class, I link being African American and being funny within historical and social structural trends. First, I highlight the ambiguous and even contradictory relationship between America's cultural goals and its social reality. I cite Klinkner and Smith (1999) in *The Unsteady March toward Racial Equality In American Society,* who contend that Americans have a strong cultural value of egalitarianism that comes from the circumstances of how we thought about ourselves relative to European elites. From the beginning of the nation, we have dealt with the contradiction between the belief that we are all equal and the knowledge that we are not. According to Klinkner and Smith, the nation has dealt most effectively with the contradiction under the following conditions: 1) when we have been at war and used black soldiers and black labor in support of the war effort, which has happened in every war, including the Revolutionary; 2) when the enemy we fought in a particular war could be demonized as the opposite of our ideals; 3) and when events that expose the contradictions in our system at home become embarrassing to the nation, for example, lynching and beatings of black soldiers after their return from defeating a racist enemy.

While Klinkner and Smith's three conditions hypothesis has been criticized, it provides an opportunity for me to interject Wilson's convergence and polarization hypothesis (1978, 1987, 2009). Whenever unsteady movement toward equality occurs, according to Wilson, two simultaneous trends are created: one in which differences between races diminish over time in the process of which race becomes a less significant social indicator, and the other in which a distinctive grouping, in this case members of a minority group, grows increasingly dissimilar from the white majority and their own minority group. In Wilson's view the latter group becomes more distinctive in language, attitudes and social beliefs while also becoming "truly disadvantaged" socially and economically.

With this sociological background in mind, I play clips of Black comedians and discuss which of Wilson's trends they may exemplify. I play a reenactment of a routine from the Chitlin circuit (Clip Twenty, Table 5.1), then a clip from the TV show *Amos and Andy* (Clip Twenty-One, Table 5.1), followed by an early TV routine performed by Mantan Moreland and Nipsey Russell (Clip Twenty-Two, Table 5.1) to illustrate the two trends.

These early performances retained and emphasized the distinctive character of being Black in America, and they also illustrated the way the comedians use cultural contradictions to generate tension for humor. Then a breakthrough actor appeared, Bill Cosby. I play his famous Noah routine from an early TV appearance (Clip Twenty-Three, Table 5.1). Of course, Cosby's portrayal of the father role helped to normalize the idea of a stable and functional family against the stereotypical dysfunctional presentation found in early Black comedy.

Lively discussion of Cosby's spoiled identity because of his criminal conviction ensued, and that provided a brief look at the raw combative humor of contemporary Black comedians such as Dave Chappell (clip Twenty-Four, Table 5.1), and a brief foray into Goffman's (1963) account of discrepancies between virtual and actual identity in the process through which one becomes discredited in modern society. While this topic warrants an entire class, I accomplish my goal by introducing students to the rich and vast sociological literature on race. The tension between inequality and equality, resistance to mainstream culture, and attacks on social structure by comedians indicate that the march goes on, even if unsteadily.

Even More Tension

I searched for more tension from which humor can be generated. The search is not difficult—simply follow the ways that social categories distinguish groups and identities. For example, regarding religion, I discovered that mega churches, the revivals, and the conventions that they hold in efforts to save souls and expand congregations, have become a circuit for Christian comedians. Just as there is Christian rock, there is also Christian humor. Much of the humor is based on resolving tension between secular and profane. Michael Jr. is one of the rare talents who crosses the line between the raw provocation of tension common on the comedy club circuit and church humor (Clip Twenty-Five, Table 5.1).

Tension among class, and what Bourdieu (1984) expanded into the concept of habitus, is well illustrated by the comedians who teamed up to put on the Blue-Collar comedy tour: Jeff Foxworthy ("You may be a redneck"), Larry the Cable Guy ("GIT-R-DONE"), Bill Engvall ("Here's Your Sign"), and Ron White ("Tater Salad") (Clip Twenty-Six, Table 5.1).

Disability humor entails resolving tension between "normal" and "aberrant," and Josh Blue, a white South African with an obvious disability, skillfully displays the tension between between an African and being disabled. Blue has a moment in his routine in which describes his birth in South America and the first look his parents got of him. The pause borders on painful. But, then he resolves the tension by saying that what they saw was a "comedian!" He then remarks that the tension he generated probably caused everyone in audience to tighten their "assholes" (Clip Twenty-Seven, Table 5.1). I also played a clip of a contemporary comedian, Chris Gethard, who uses the topics of depression and suicide to generate humor. He speaks openly about his own background and his feeling about making these subjects part of his standup routine (Clip Twenty-Eight, Table 5.1).

Williams, in his classic text, *American Society: A Sociological Interpretation* (1970), depicts the dynamics that are created whenever ideal cultural goals and actual social practices are in conflict. He suggested that at least two outcomes are possible: first, norms of evasion develop which function to maintain both the ideal and the practice. There are too many to enumerate; perhaps the most obvious is the "war on drugs." After more than forty years of war, drugs are still plentiful and cheap, and politicians get elected on the promise to rid society of drugs. Or, as Williams stated, the goals and values become consistent with practices by virtue of changes in one or the other. For example, civil rights and various manifestation of feminism demonstrate the drive toward consistency.

Can humor function as a kind of norm of evasion? This question provides an opportunity to discuss the limits of taste in humor, the conflict between uncensored comic expression and "approved" expression of it. Lenny Bruce's routines that included profanity, George Carlin's words you can't say on television, all can be part of the discussion of "ways around" established norms.

Sarcasm and Modernity

While satire and irony are hallmarks of Western literature and story-telling, sarcasm is a relatively new kid on the block (Haiman 1998). Sarcasm is an ironic or satirical remark that seems to be praising someone or something but is really taunting or cutting. Sarcasm can be used to hurt or offend or can be used for comic affect. Just few examples: I'm trying to imagine you with a personality. I work 40 hours a week to be this poor. Well, this day was a total waste of makeup. This isn't an office. It's Hell with fluorescent lighting. Don't bother me. I'm living happily ever after. Sarcasm depends on intonation and other para-linguistic devices So, to use it in text, for instance, in social media or email, the sarcmark was invented. (Illustrations of the sarcmark are widely available on the Internet).

Haiman, in his book, *Talk Is Cheap: Sarcasm, Alienation, and the Evolution of Language* (1998), suggests that sarcasm is an adaptation to the complexity of life in modern society. With increased alienation in a given society, we see more and more sophisticated sarcasm. As an utterance that carries a meta-meaning, sarcasm might be the way to talk in complicated interactive setting with strangers, and most likely with friends tied together through negotiated links. This means that interactive settings are constantly changing and demand constant updating to stay salient.

> Our culture in particular is permeated with sarcasm. People who don't understand sarcasm are immediately noticed. They're not getting it. They're not socially adept (Hurley, Dan, "The Science of Sarcasm (Not That You Care)" *New York Times*, June 3, 2008).

Sarcasm saturates twenty-first-century America. According to one study of a database of telephone conversations, 23 percent of the time that the phrase "yeah, right" was used, it was uttered sarcastically (Chin 2011). Entire phrases have almost lost their literal meanings because they are so frequently said with a sneer. "Big deal," for example. "My heart bleeds for you." There might be a case for sarcasm according to the linguists (Haiman 1998) and neuroscientists (Rankin 2009). For example, they suggest that exposure to sarcasm enhances creative problem solving. Children understand and use sarcasm by the time they get to kindergarten. An inability to understand sarcasm may be an early warning sign of brain disease or autistic tendencies. Sarcasm exercises the brain more than sincere statements do. Sarcasm appears to stimulate complex thinking and to attenuate the otherwise negative effects of anger. It promotes a "theory of the mind" that allows recognition that you don't literally mean what you say, and this works only if your listener gets that you're insincere. Sarcasm has a two-faced quality: it's both funny and mean.

After this perusal of research on sarcasm, I document declining trends of trust in institutions in America, using Gallup and General Social Survey data (for example, Table 5.2). Pointing to an association between the complexity of life in modern society and types of humor (sarcmark), I illustrate the use of sarcasm in humor by showing Clip Twenty-Nine (Table 5.1) of Jerry Seinfeld on *The Tonight Show*. Seinfeld's sarcastic description of the US Postal Service complements his critique of the self-centered use of cell phones. Like a French king, the cell phone user scrolls thorough his contacts to select whom he shall visit today.

Table 5.2.   Percent of Adult Americans with Great Deal of Confidence in Institutions by Year (GSS)

	Year	
Institutions	*1972*	*2016*
Scientific Community	40%	40%
Organized Religion	36%	20%
Organized Labor	36%	20%
Congress	24%	6%
Public Education	37%	26%
Supreme Court	32%	26%
Major Companies	31%	18%
Press	25%	8%

CONCLUSIONS AND DIRECTIONS

To tie together the disparate aspects of humor, I turn to a discussion of the social functions. The following generalizations serve as platforms for identifying specific functions from the various clips played. Humor within a group and sometimes even laughter, can function to create a distinctive group atmosphere, lessen tension, narrow conflicts, build cohesion, and maintain a hierarchy of norms. Between group and society, humor can act as a social corrective, as a means of attack on culture and society.

Any application of functional theory requires a quick introduction to Merton's concept of latent dysfunction (Merton 1957). I referred to his famous two-by-two table (function/dysfunction by manifest/latent) that worked well to point out examples from the clips previously shown. Then, I suggest that a treatment of humor must take a comparative perspective to fully appreciate the role that context, both macro and micro, play in generating humor. There seems to be little comparative sociology of humor, so I suggest a heuristic device: namely to characterize societies by their degree of fragmentation (high or low) and their social control structures (autocratic or democratic). For purposes of discussion, I select exemplars and then postulate the type of humor that a particular set of social conditions might foster. I rely on McGraw and Warner's (2014) account of their travels to uncover the secrets of humor to flesh out examples of humor in the various countries (see Table 5.3).

Table 5.3. Varieties of Humor by Societal Types

High Fragmentation, Hierarchical Control	Low Fragmentation, Democratic Control
Fatalist, Physical Palestine	Cartoon Controversy Sweden, Denmark
High Fragmentation, Democratic Control	Low Fragmentation, Hierarchical Control
Standup, Sarcasm United States, UK	Ritualized, Escapist Japan

I summarized the materials covered in the following way. As a species, we seem particularly adapted to laughing, and laughter seems to be based in our evolutionary history. The most basic stimuli for laughter are physical and visual humor. Linguistic humor is universal but obviously is relative to the social and cultural text of a given audience. I review for the class the role that social categories play in humor, emergence of sarcasm and narratives of everyday life.

I enjoyed teaching the sociology of humor, and while Life Quest does not have a formal teacher evaluation procedure, I did receive compliments and criticisms. In particular, this class of seniors expressed a limited tolerance for what they regarded as the overuse of expletives by contemporary comedians. Our discussion about expletives was spirited, so much so that I spent a few minutes discussing a scholarly analysis of the use of expletives (Seizer 2011). Seizer suggests that obscene language use functions as a timing and rhythm device in standup routines, and this allows a comedian to establish rapport with young audiences. Needless to say, such analysis did little to change attitudes in that older adult class about the excessive use of expletives in modern comedy. A particularly flattering compliment came from a retired college English teacher who told me that he had taught humor in literature many times but had difficulty not "killing the frog." He told me that I had successfully kept the frog alive.

I relate my experiences in teaching with the intention to inspire others to utilize the power of YouTube to enliven classrooms with visual and auditory illustrations of sociological concepts. I share the clips I found useful, but my selections are merely suggestive. Internet based sharing, especially YouTube, offers great promise for connecting with students, both old and young.

NOTES

1. Parts of this chapter were previously published in *Michigan Journal of Sociology* 34 (2020): 106–128.

2. https://ualr.edu/atle/2011/01/24/teaching-workshop-by-JeffreyNash/.

Part III

The chapters in Part Three have a common implicit theme. They show how deeply embedded meanings occur in social contexts that are invariably local. Each chapter rests on an acknowledgment that it is crucial to know meanings in their local contexts before fully analyzing a structural topic such as animal rights, abortion, environment concerns and public sociology. As a colleague remarked, these chapters express the "local to global" idea.

Being the target of animal rights groups, and just exploring the history of a breed of dog, sets the stage for my understanding of the ways that perennial questions get answered. For example, which forms of life are worth saving, and where is the balance between the welfare of human beings and that of animals. In chapter Six, we learn that the answers that people have to these questions depends in large measure on where they live, with whom they associate and how integrated they are in the structures of society, that is, the intersections of their lives.

In chapter Seven is the story of resisting the construction of a coal plant and the discovery that macro-level policy and practice both reflects and exploits local communities. As Scott McNall insists, local involvements are crucial for building the kind of bridges needed for effective social movements. The plant was built, but resistance to it teaches a lesson that local knowledge, involvement, and participation are essential to building a bridge between environmental activism and the affairs of everyday life.

In chapter Eight, my devotion to a sociological life leads to the movement sponsored by the American Sociological Association called public sociology. I relate how personal sociology interacts with public sociology, and how it transformed me into an editorial opinion writer.

Chapter Six

Lives Worth Saving

The Moral Paradox of Life

A colleague and I were having lunch and she told me about returning home the day before to find graffiti on her retaining wall and signs on her yard calling her husband a pig killer and demanding the liberation of the lab animals he uses in his research at the nearby university. Neither of us knew much about the animal rights movement, but I had just published an article on bulldogs (at the time, a proud owner the English bulldog, Sir Bernard Spike) as cultural objects and she, an anthropologist, was interested in cultural variations in the roles that animals play in society. We had published a paper on changing ways of thinking about animal human interactions (Sutherland and Nash 1994), and the parallel logics with the pro-life movement struck us.

We decided to compare the belief systems of pro-life people with those of animal right activists. What seems to be a logical dilemma for both belief systems actually might create solidarity and defensive arguments for each system. This chapter is based on our interviews with animal rights activists and survey data from the General Social Survey. It is personal in sense that our lives were challenged by these beliefs, and we wanted to understand how such strong commitments to beliefs function in everyday life.

Nearly a third of the adult American population believes that animals have the same moral rights as human beings, which presumably means the right to live. At least, that is the way they responded to a question about whether they thought animals have the same moral rights as human beings (see GSS 1993, 1994 and 2000). In some nations such a Japan, Poland, Russia, and Germany, the percentage attributing moral rights to animals is very high. In Japan, that percentage is 77 percent according to the 2000 International Social Survey Program. A smaller but still significant number believe that these rights include not being slaughtered as food for human consumption and protecting animals from medical experimentation.

No small logical step to the immorality of factory farming animals (chickens, pigs and cattle), and the assertion that humans do not have the moral right to take the lives of higher order living things. The animal rights movement, as it is often referred to, has a rich and rather long history, and it has proven its effectiveness to protect animals and extent their welfare through laws and ordinances.

The pro-life movement offers another moral version of life. Adherents of this movement believe in the sanctity of human life to a degree unknown before advances in medical technology and practice that identify, prolong and sustain life. Extreme proponents of pro-life beliefs define human life as beginning at conception and regard any form of abortion as "murder."

In the same society, we can find people who extend moral rights, if not obligations, to animals, and may go the great extremes to promote their view of "life," and another group of people, equally passionate and adamant, who want to extend moral and legal protection to a form of developing life they call the "unborn." These two groups of people have highly developed senses of morality, consisting of systems of belief that they have learned, passed on to others and refined into eloquent narratives about life, its sanctity, and, most important, the individual's obligations to protect life. How can one group, the pro-animalist, think a mother should have the legal to terminate a "life," while the other, the pro-life, seems to have no moral version of the sanctity of life for any form of life other than their own? How does one understand what seems to be a paradox: Animals rightist favor the legal right of a mother to terminate a pregnancy, but not the killing of animals for food, or the use of animals for medical testing. Pro-life proponents regard the termination of a pregnancy as "murder, "yet, they do not object to factory farming of animals or hunting in all its manifestations. Obviously, the two groups have defined "life" in very distinctive ways.

CONTRADICTIONS?

How do we sorts pieces of this paradox into categories. The first step is to look for board similarities among the people who espouse these views. Can we characterize animal rightist and pro-lifers according the some general categories? Early attempts to do this categorization suggested an outline that can be filled in with some detail.

Who are animal rightist? The animal rights movement had its start more than a century ago, when values and beliefs about animals and their place in society began to change. For example, the British parliament banned "bull baiting" in 1835 as a "medieval and cruel" sport. "Bull baiting" was popular betting sport among the common people. It consisted of staking down in the town square a bull where dogs, specially bred for the battle, where set on the bull. Wagers were made on all aspects of the combat between dogs and bulls. By the middle of the nineteenth century, urban middle classes were increasingly offended by this practice and were able to use their new founded political power to pass legislation outlawing the practice (Nash 1989). Already, we can see that beliefs about the treatment of animals can be placed in a social context. In the case of "bull baiting," commoners who practiced and supported their "sport," and the middle classes and intellectuals who found the "sport" vulgar and barbaric. One cannot help but notice similar class perspectives on the "sports" of cock and dog fighting—still popular among some classes of people, while abhorrent to others.

Perhaps the first scientific study to attempt to characterize proanimal rightist was the study conducted by Jasper and Nelkin (1991). They capitalized on an unprecedented event, The March for the Animals, which took place in Washington, DC in the summer of 1990. That march was sponsored by a number of organizations that purport to support animal rights, including PETA and the Alliance for Animal Legislation. They interviewed 412 participants in the march. Their data indicated that

> Typical respondents were Caucasian, highly educated urban professional women approximately thirty years old with a median income of $33,000 (1989). Most activists think of themselves as Democrats or as Independents, and have moderate to liberal political views. They were often suspicious of science and made no distinctions between basic and applied science, or public versus private animal-based research. The research suggests that animal rights activism is in part a symbolic manifestation of egalitarian social and political views concerning scientific and technological change. (Jamison and Lunch 1992, 438)

The General Social Survey (GSS) took note of the activism of the animal rights and included three items as part of its omnibus survey of the adult American population in 1993 and 1994. They asked a representative sample if they agreed with the statements "Animals should have the same moral rights that human beings do" and "Animals should be used in medical testing if it saves human lives" and whether they themselves "refused to eat meat for moral reasons." The GSS includes a wide range of questions that permit researchers to depict the social characteristics of people who agree or disagree with these statements. Several articles have been published that deal directly with the whether there is a profile for people with proanimal beliefs.

For example, women are more likely than men to express proanimal sentiments. This is particularly so for the question about moral rights, less for testing using animals and refusing to eat meat. Taking social characteristics one at a time shows, young people, those with a relatively high level of education, city dwellers, and middle-class people express proanimal sentiments. As is often the case in social science research, there is a debate about the underlying causes of these patterns.

Two interpretations seem to capture the gist of the arguments. On the one hand, are those who see proanimal sentiments as associated with new values emerging out of sweeping social transformations, that is, conditions of social life have changed so dramatically for those of us who live in "developed" societies that we are forming new ways of thinking about our relationships with animals and, more generally, with our environment. Traditional views such as those rooted in Biblical views of God-given human dominion over all things on earth are being replaced by views that are far less homocentric. Some refer to the value shift as the raise of post-materialism (Inglehart 1997) others as postmodernism (Bauman 2005).

Still others suggest that the social movements often influence what people think about issues in subtle yet effective ways. For example, whenever a social movement gains enough momentum to attract national attention (television, news, and even books), its basic ideas often work their way into common talk. Over time, even if the core beliefs of the movement are not shared by the majority of society, these beliefs become part of a national discourse, at least in the sense they are recognized and articulated.

Public opinion pollsters have traced the diffusion of attitudes toward animals, and found that, in the United States, proanimal sentiments have "lukewarm" support (Gallup, May 21, 2003). The vast majority of Americans say that

> animals deserve some protection from harm and exploitation, and a quarter say animals deserve the same protection as human beings. But most Americans oppose banning medical research and product testing on laboratory animals . . . [and are strongly opposed to banning hunting] . . . Women are more likely than men to support animal rights, Democrats more than Republicans, but there are few differences by age.

Some researchers have objected to any attempt at profiling those with proanimal attitudes. For example, Jerolmack (2003) analyzed general social survey data and found little support for what he refers to as "stereotypes" of those who support animal rights. He attacks, after performing logistic statistical analysis on the 1993 and 1994 GSS data, the "stereotypical" profile of an animal rights supporter as female, well educated, upper-middle class, middle-aged and white.

> The data in this study do not support the stereotype. Instead the young non-black minorities, and the less educated were more likely to support animal rights;

income was not a significant predictor . . . This study findings suggest the need to rethink "post-materialist" and "post-citizenship" theories about who supports animal rights. (2003, 245)

However, analyzing these same data, I found a significant relationship between a kind of engagement with society and the likelihood of expressing proanimal sentiments. My analysis points more toward a post-modern interpretation of these beliefs. Attitudes extending "human" qualities to animals and affording them protection and status equivalent to humans might be associate with larger changes in society. As the daily lives of people change from close and enduring interaction with family and community to distance and fleeting relationships with larger numbers of strangers, and as disengagement from traditional institutional life continues, sharp and traditional distinctions between animals and humans might also change.

Lively questions exist about the degree and quality of changes in the core networks that define social life for Americans (Putnam 2000). One way to characterize this change is as two extremes—one comprised of social ties grounded in core institutions, such as family, religion and politics (these are the three avenues for what the classic sociologist, Emile Durkheim, called social integration). The other is made up of networks of friends, peers, interest groups, leisure time activities; in short, people with whom one might share an interest, skill, or some concern that brings them together around a specific activity. James Coleman (1993) called the first type of network institutional or primordial and the second constructed or associational. Similar trends have been documented for the effects of religion on the selection of marriage partners. Traditional boundaries have weakened as more fluid and opportunistic forces replace them.

Currently, the social boundaries that separate educational groups seem to be stronger than the boundaries that separate Protestants and Catholics. In addition, there is some evidence that interfaith marriages have become increasingly homogenous with respect to education, suggesting that education has replaced religion as a factor in spouse selection. (Kalmijn 1991)

There can be little doubt that the pace and demands of everyday life in contemporary society have had a scattering effect on social life. We deal more superficially and tangentially with large numbers of people about whom we know little, and, at the same time, we seem to be retreating in small worlds of people we trust. McPherson, Smith-Lovin, and Brashears (2006), using data that span a twenty-year period, show that Americans have fewer confidants (people with whom they might discuss serious matters) in 2004 than they did in 1985. Their analysis points to increased isolation in general and a tendency for people to cluster with others of similar background. A picture emerges of a diverse society where people deal in a cursory manner with those different from themselves while retreating in a smaller circle of people who matter to them.

Under these conditions, it is quite possible for people to politely or, in disinterested ways, dismiss the points of view others; and, by talking only to those of like minds and hearts, maintain increasingly parochial views. While these tendencies seem ironic, unraveling their meanings helps to understand how they sustain and inform everyday beliefs.

Is it true that people whose lives, wrapped up in constructed or associational social ties, are more likely to be proanimal that those who are institutionally related? To test the idea that people who are disengaged from institutional life are the ones who are more proanimal in attitude, we constructed several indicators of social integration which we take to be the degree to which involvement with others is reflected in social life.

Using GSS data, we coded variables that measure family life giving the highest score to those currently married with the largest number of children, and the lowest score to people who were unmarried without children. Our indicator of religious life is a sum of the variables of belief in God, how people classified their beliefs (fundamental, moderate, or liberal), and their views of the Bible as the "actual word" of God, "inspired word," or as "an ancient book." We, also, counted how frequently they attended church. We assessed political integration through the construction of a simple proxy using voting in the last presidential election. (This indicator has an observed range from 2 to 33. Fitting the observed distribution against a normal curve, according to a goodness-of-fit test, suggests the data are normally distributed (KSL Test, $p < .01$).

Using our indicator of traditional social integration as a predictor of whether a person would agree that animals have the same moral rights as humans, we discovered that, indeed, men and women different in the likelihood of being proanimal, but that our indicator predicted agreement for both men and women with the statement that animals have moral rights. For example, the probability that a male with a very low integration score would agree with the statement about moral rights for animals was nearly 50 percent, while a male with high integration score was only about 10 percent likely to agree. The percentages for women were over 60 percent for those with low integration scores to about 50 percent for those with very high scores. While the gender difference does seem to be significant (see Gallup, "Gender gap in Support for Animal Rights, but no Significant Generational Differences" 2004), our analysis points to a trend, the decline in institutional social life that seems to be affecting both genders.

Analyses such as this one are fraught with difficulties. The meanings that people attribute to statements can be notoriously idiosyncratic, contexts can change over time, and different researchers may code or interpret data differently. Still, the reader can check on whether a measure of traditional integration predicts response to the question on moral rights by conducting his or her own analysis. Using multiple and logit regression, I found that variables measuring involvement in family and religious life do have a relationship with proanimal sentiments. These technical analyses involve assessing the combined effects of several variables on a single dependent variable. In this case how a person answered the question of moral rights was the dependent variable. The variables that consistently helped predict how a person responded were church attendance, the number children the person had, their marital status, and whether they saw the Bible as the actual word of God. Both multiple and logit regression models were significant explaining about 10 percent of the variance in the responses. Such a finding is hardly solid proof of a causal relationship, but it does suggest that a postmodern interpretation of beliefs about the morality of animals might be appropriate.

Therefore, there may be some merit in looking for a link between social changes and institutional decline and the raise of thinking of animals in human terms.

One possible solution to confusing animals with humans is to recognize an irony. It appears the people whose lives are closest to nature, that is, farmers and others who deal directly with land and animals are most likely to see essential differences between animals and human beings. People whose lives are remote from direct contact with nature, who experience nature virtually or through relationships with companion animals are most likely to blur the distinctions between animals and human beings, and most often, this blur takes the form of moving animals towards humans and not vice a versa.

We arrive at an insight not far from that of the classic sociologist, Emile Durkhiem, who was concerned about the moral consequences of rapid social change (see Tomasi 2000). Observing what was happening to his native France, especially to the moral fabric of society as reflected in an alarming increase in suicides, he attempted to link a variety of problems to the degree and nature of the transformations that France was experiencing. Over one hundred years ago, these changes were urbanization, industrialization, greater mobility of families and migration. These trends he linked to excessive individualism, alienation and anomie, and even reactionary mass movements.

Today, our society is also undergoing a great transformation that portent ominous changes. The meanings of marriages change under the pressure of increased longevity; communications, mass and otherwise. Our lives become even more fast paced that the "New York minute" of the early twenty-first century. Today, most events and our experience of them become hyper (witness the opening and closing ceremonies of the Beijing Olympics). Distinctions between animals, machine, and humans blur in towers of robot-looking human beings moving in mechanical waves up and around a tower. Not only are old meanings changed, but the old seems woefully inadequate to depict what is happening.

I grew up attending a Southern Baptist church. As a teenager, I seriously thought I was called to the ministry (that is how the decision to become a Baptist minister is referred to). I attended and graduated from Baylor University, the world's largest and perhaps best-known Baptist university. It has been nearly thirty years since I have been to church service or a Sunday school class in a Baptist church. Over a Christmas vacation several years ago, I spent three weeks with my younger sister and her husband in Florida. She and he had retained lifetime ties with the Baptist church. As their guest, I found myself going to services, singing with their church choir and attending Sunday school. This was just after the presidential election in which George Bush defeated John Kerry. I heard congratulations about the reelection of George W. Bush, and I learned that this church actually taught a class prior to the election which profiled candidates for local, state, and national offices according to their "Christian" values. While the classes were careful not of endorse a particular candidate, it was clear that believers were expected to vote for those closest to their beliefs. This was not the separation-of-church-and-state Baptists I recalled from my youth. I asked myself "What has changed?" High technology in the form of sound systems, video displays and Power Point presentations did not exist when I was Baptist. And, I have vivid memories of hearing sermons from the pulpit of First Baptist Church in 1960 about the danger to the nation that the election of a Catholic president would bring. But it seems to me that one big change has occurred. I have no recall of discussion of the issue of abortion. The process was illegal and never acknowledged, especially not in church.

Abortion is a flash point issue, a wedge that separates Americans on a very fundamental, culturally sensitive set of meanings. Although Gallup polls shows that the issue is of relative importance to American voters, beliefs about abortion are clearly tangled up with religious beliefs and cultural values. Tamney, Johnson, and Burton (1992) use data from the Middletown study to confirm that attitudes about abortion are linked to variation in cultural beliefs and values:

> the acceptance of legalized abortion among Americans is a consequence of individualism which finds expression in libertarian and feminist ideologies. On the

other hand, opposition to legalized abortion finds its ideological justification in the religious tradition, specifically in natural law or puritanical doctrines. (34)

Through the application of a sophisticated statistical analysis of the results of the Middletown survey, they found that support for legalized abortion was related to a commitment to privacy, a belief that human life begins at conception, and social traditionalism. The importance of religion in determining abortion attitudes was also substantiated (43). However, they qualified their findings by showing that, to a degree, attitudes toward all life are related negatively to favoring legalized abortion. In Catholic circles, the view that all life must be persevered is referred to as the "seamless garment" doctrine. Political conservatism was positively related to opposition to legalized abortion but only for the more highly educated in the sample. Social traditionalism, which they defined as anti-public school sex education, opposition of sexual freedom and pornography and beliefs that women's place is in the home, was related to anti-abortion views for conservative protestants, but less so for Catholics.

According to this research, "the debate about legalized abortion is a battleground for people possessing different values." Individualists and traditionalists are pitted against one another in this conflict. Traditionalists are committed to the puritanical moral tradition, while political conservatives emphasize the need for tradition as the basis for social order. Others seem influenced by "natural law," and seek to prevent human manipulation of innocent life. Religion is clearly an important influence in the cultural context within which the abortion debate takes place (Tamney, Johnson, and Burton 1992).

In perhaps the most influential study of concepts of life, Luker (1984) offered a characterization of women for whom the issue of abortion is consuming. They are the activists, both for and against abortion. For them, abortion is a symbolic issue that pits two world views against one another. The issue of "life," when it begins and what it means, divides women as no other issue. Luker argues that the current abortion controversy is over more than the personhood of the fetus. It pits two very different groups of women with very different world views against each other. An important distinction is their views of motherhood. Pro-life women favor restrictions on abortion as an affirmation of motherhood as the most important role a woman can play. Pro-choice women treat abortion as a right through which they affirm that "motherhood, while certainly a good thing, is a private, discretionary choice that women may well want to forego or delay in favor of doing something else" (Himmelstein, 1986).

Luker links these different values placed on motherhood to the interests of groups of women who inhabit very different social works. Pro-choice women disproportionately work in the paid labor force and have high-status professional, managerial, and business jobs. They have high levels of education and good personal incomes. They are more likely than pro-life women to be either single or divorced and to have small families. Pro-life women, in contrast, are more likely to be housewives with larger families. If they do work in the paid labor force, it is at lower-status, traditionally female jobs. They have little or no personal income and fewer years of schooling than the pro-choice women.

Luker is careful to show that interests and values are not simply derived from location in different social worlds. While women define different interests that lead to different values regarding motherhood and family roles, they also act on their beliefs and values. Pro-life women chose marriage and family over education and career because they already valued family roles very highly; pro-choice chose education and career because of different values. Values and interests influence each other. In his review of Luker's book, Himmelstein writes about this interest and value relationship:

> The common theme here is opposition to too much individual autonomy, too much freedom from constraints imposed by traditional roles and norms, too much emphasis on individual self-determination and self-fulfillment. It implies a Pro-life worldview in which individualism in itself is suspect and constraint in itself valued. (470–71)

The people who make up our society do have very distinct and seemingly contradictory beliefs and values about the most fundamental questions. Those who move their interpretation of the values of animal life towards a more anthropomorphic view might be more autonomous (individualistic) and less traditional than the active pro-lifers who seem less concerned about animals than with what a fetus symbolizes. Likewise, the lives of animals for those most heavily involved in that movement stand for more. They symbolize a dissatisfaction with life in general in contemporary society. Saving animals is a proxy for saving the earth and for a way of life less harried. more harmonious with a view of gentle and sustaining nature.

But these beliefs and values are just that—matters of the mind and heart. All such matters are common to us all. The key is in understanding that the variation in beliefs and values is not random. Instead, the distribution can be depicted in such a way that we can see how seemingly paradoxical questions resolve into a pattern.

To appreciate how seemingly unrelated social movements are linked both at the level of belief and organization, we rely on Erikson's concept of "axis of variation," and suggest that the power and influence of these movements derives from their contradictory relations to a core value—the preservation of life. Erikson proposes that we recognize that contradiction is part of the "cultural order of things," and that culture consists only of core values but of "lines of point and counterpoint along which they diverge" (1976, 81). Along axes of variation are patterns of actions, thoughts, feelings, and imaginations that operate at both the collective and individual level. And, we can expect that the structure of particular groups will embody the contradictions, tension and emotional meanings of the total culture.

If we take "animals rights" and "pro-life" as ends of an axis of American culture that is concerned with meanings of life itself, we can identify variation in belief and competing social integration along this axis. We can, also, define "gradients along which responses to social change are likely to take place" (Erikson 1976, 83). The respective movements and what proponents believe and value become polar alternatives for defining the meanings of life itself and for participation in society.

While believers often seem impervious to criticism that point out logical fallacies in their thinking, they follow a "logic-in-action" formula that shapes the meanings they impute to what they say and do. We can depict these logics for each pole of the axis (see Figure 6.1). Proanimal believers follow a secular and individualistic logic based these premises: 1) naturally occurring things are essentially good, 2) human beings are the sources of harm, 3) animals are natural and, therefore, animals are naturally superior to humans. 4) However, animals are seriously disadvantaged in the unnatural world of human beings.

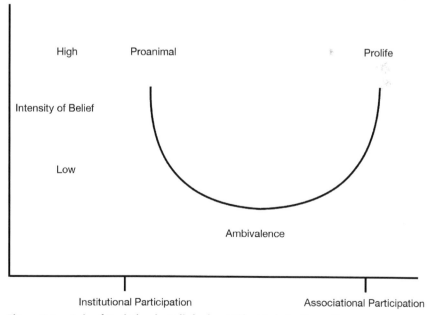

Figure 6.1.   Axis of Variation in Beliefs about Life. Made by the author.

Hence, 5) humans have an obligation to defend animals since they, the human beings, have altered nature.

Defense of animals and acting as spokesperson for animals offers redemption from human failings. The plight of animals serves as a symbol of human failings and holds up a model for human good. A fetus is thought of as within the scope of responsibility that a woman has over her own body. The cognitive powers of the individual can trump "natural" character of life. While survey research shows that responses to the question "Do animals have the same moral rights as humans" is not associated with how a person response to the question, "Should a woman have a legal right to an abortion for any reason?" among those who believe that animals should has the same moral rights as human, 45 percent are pro-choice (General Social Survey, years 93 and 94, n= 1,439).

Pro-life believers follow a logic that is sacred, shared, and built on these premises: 1) Life is divine gift, 2) humans are uniquely divine-like, 3) humans are subject to divine design, 4) human dominion over animals is divine, 5) human life begins at conception, and 6) animal life is less divine than human. *The human fetus symbolizes way of life, in which divine trumps secular.* The issue of rights for animals plays an insignificant role in the thought process of pro-lifers. Animals may be "members of the family," but they do not carry the symbolic power of human life. Hence, issues of eating meat, advocating on behalf of animals simply do not fit into the logical framework.

My analysis of GSS data shows that involvement in the traditional institutions of society is associated with beliefs about life. Such an observation helps us locate beliefs and values within a social context and leads to an understanding of how thinking about life can include and exclude distinct meanings.

René Descartes is often vivified in proanimal literature as the origin of a false distinction between animals and humans. His stress on the cognitive capability of humans set humans and animals in different domains. Today, scholars reject that distinction by showing the animals, even dogs and cats, are capable of cognition and emotion more like human than previously thought. Some have even advocated that long standing traditions in the study of the social self be extended to companion animals (Irving 2004).

If the distinctions between animals and humans becomes increasingly blurred, there may be implications for the way pro-lifers and proanimal proponents decide what their positions should be. Could pro-lifers see the divinity in animals and proanimalist see the animal in the unborn? Perhaps, and with increasing changes in modes and quality of social associations, in a postmodern sense, affiliations and ties can shifts like water (Bauman 2005). When the liquid runs a particular current, we might even understand Descartes's devotion to his little dog, Monsieur Grat.

Chapter Seven

A Coal-Fired Plant Is Born (with Dina Nash)

My wife, Dina, and I have been environmental activists for some time. We have marched, written letters to senators and representatives, spoken at public meetings of the state regulatory agencies, and she has served in various offices in environmental organizations. Dina was honored by a state-wide organization as the environmental activist of the year, and she served for a time as the main volunteer organizer for the movement to stop the construction of the John W. Turk coal plant in Arkansas. I, being more academic, have followed closely the development of the sociology of environment.

Books I found influential on the sociology of environment include Foster, Clark, and Yory's work, The *Ecological Rift: Capitalism's War on the Earth* (2010), and McNall's *Rapid Climate Change* (2011). While I don't consider environmental sociology a specialty of mine, I am engaged in promoting public understanding of climate change and its impact on everyday health and social life.

When we learned that a 600-megawatt coal fired plant was to be built in a pristine rural region of southwest Arkansas, not far from the birthplace of former President William J. Clinton, we joined in the effort to stop it. We drove to Hope, Arkansas for two of several public hearings that the power company held. One of America's largest power companies, American Electric Power's subsidiary Southwestern Electric Power Company, was behind the plan. Eventually, the plant was built and was, to date, the most expensive electric project in Arkansas history at 1.8 billion dollars. The story of the siting of the Turk plant, the regulatory approval process and our experience of that process, reveals some fundamental truths about how "things happen" in America. And provided yet another opportunity for personal sociology.

As this story unfolds, two observations support the details of what happened. First, energy companies have elaborate schemes for deciding where to site power plants. Using social science methods, they search for a location where there has been population decline, poverty, isolation from major urban areas, and low levels of education among the local population. Their models suggest places where local resistance to the construction of a power plant will be low. Fulton, Arkansas, fits the criteria to a tee. And, in the uncovering of the practices of "Big Coal," we learned that personal and political matters interact with scientific ones, and at other times they directly determine policy and practice. We read the book, *Big Coal: The Dirty Secret Behind America's Energy Future* by Jeff Goodell (2006) and Dina wrote a summary of research on health effects of burning fossil fuels from the Industrial Revolution to 2008.

Second, as we became more involved in the movement to stop the coal plant, we noticed that how people talked about the issues reflected their beliefs and values, which showed the way they understood, either in supportive or oppositional ways, the significance of the coal plant.

We wondered how local residents could believe the claims of Big Coal that their community members would enjoy high paying jobs, that schools would benefit from property taxes that the plant would pay, and that the hunting club opposing the plant could be sure their duck habitat would be protected. Actually, most of the ongoing high-paying jobs at the plant will be filled by engineers from outside the community, while the lower-paid maintenance jobs could be boiler-makers trained at Hope Community College. The jobs to construct the plant would last two years and usually, crews of such builders hired by AEP would come from out of state and use only the minimum of local folks who had dump trucks or dirt to sell. While property taxes would benefit the local schools, the long-term standard of living for most residents would not improve, and their health would be quite negatively impacted, raising the respiratory miseries such as asthma and early deaths from other coal-related diseases. Locals talked about the plant as a way to slow the exodus of young citizens who presumably would find new economic vitality in the local towns and settle nearby. A manager from another SWEPCO plant fed into their hopes by talking about maintenance jobs and good salaries, ignoring the health impacts on the community. When we spoke to him privately after a hearing, asking how many people it will kill prematurely, he did not admit to knowing about any health impacts.

Our reading of the impact of the coal plant suggests that communities gain a little in the short run from the construction of the plant, but stand to lose much in the long run. Still, as an African American mayor of the one of smaller townships near the proposed site said at a public hearing, "We need this plant desperately." Another elderly gentleman and long-time resident of the area said, "They can build the thing in my back yard if they want to!"—a reverse of the NIMBY effect.

And, according to the power company behind the plant, about 30 or so jobs were created to run and maintain the plant. In the end, the Turk coal plant did not stop the migration of young people from small towns to cities.

Opponents of the plant, mostly from environmental organizations, along with two game and fish officers worried about the negative impact of air quality on animals and destruction of the view of nature, and one local doctor, talked about ominous predictions of pollution, health risks, and climate change. Mercury and other byproducts from the burning of coal, they say, permanently harm the pristine swamp waters, lakes with alligators, and many species of fish and birds. The locals, except for the doctor, didn't seem to know or care much about the negative impacts on air and health. Particulate pollution was not in the local awareness, and since the concept was brought in mostly by us "foreigners," it did not sink in.

How can the same plant be seen in such polarized terms? How can views of it, its effects, and its significance for the community and the surrounding region, be so opposite? We looked at how story telling or what academics refer to as narrative convention provides the key to understanding how the plant can have so many different meanings to so many different people.

We failed to stop the coal plant. The John Turk Plant began generating electricity and burning coal in 2012 after years of litigation, first begun by a hunting club near the plant's site, joined later by the national and state Sierra Club and the Audubon Society. Here's a brief account of the litigation that went on after the public input hearings and the plant's approval by the Arkansas Department of Environmental Quality:

Though first proposed in 2006, lawsuits aiming to protect the environment surrounding the project's proposed site delayed its groundbreaking. Plaintiffs cited potential damage to the area's fish, wildlife, grasslands, and cypress and hardwood groves. As part of a settlement reached in December 2011 with the Sierra Club, the National Audubon Society, Audubon Arkansas and the Hempstead County Hunting Club, American Electric Power/SWEPCO agreed to close one of the 528 megawatt generating units at its J. Robert Welsh Power Plant in Texas by the end of 2016 and purchase 400 megawatts of renewable energy capacity by the end of 2014. The settlement also required the company to contribute $8 million to The Nature Conservancy, $2 million to the Arkansas Community Foundation, and reimburse $2 million in legal fees. American Electric Power/ SWEPCO agreed to never install additional generating units at the plant or build another coal-fired facility within 30 miles. SWEPCO announced in January of 2012 it had reached 20-year agreements to purchase 359 megawatts of wind power from sources in Oklahoma, Texas, and Kansas, more than quadrupling its wind power portfolio. The Oklahoma Municipal Power Authority, a 7 percent owner of the Turk plant, entered a 25-year agreement in 2012 to purchase 49 megawatts of wind power capacity. (Adapted from websites, May 1, 2021)

So, we tried, and if belatedly, so did Sierra and Audubon, the hunt club, and others who joined as parties to the litigation, and while there were concessions mostly in the form of money, the Turk plant continues to operate as the pride of SWEPCO: it's ultra-supercritical "clean coal plant." What's left for a sociologist but to retell and extract sociological observations, to see the plant sociologically. Doing so requires that we look for narrative themes and ways that those who create these meanings are personally involved in the telling.

TALES OF COAL

One way to talk about the plant is through the lens of global warming or climate change. We've all seen movies about the melting of the North Pole ice and the fate of the polar bear. We've heard lectures on the same happening in Antarctica. Who can forget *Inconvenient Truth* with Al Gore dangling on the top of a cherry picker illustrating the rise in CO2 and the projected rise in global temperature on what has to be the world's largest line graph? Just search the Internet and you'll find maps showing where seawater will flood homes and streets, given various increases in global temperature. What are we going do with all those displaced people?

Some people seem to have the topic on their minds all the time. Others just don't want to talk about at all. We've heard people in their seventies say they don't care, since at our age we won't be around to see the forecasted disasters. When we reply, "What about your children and grandchildren?" They often don't have a comeback, or they deny the hypothesis of humanly induced climate change, or they express some optimistic vision of yet to be developed technologies and sources of energy that will mitigate the predicted catastrophes.

What seem to be at the root of all the talk are competing visions of the future. When an issue emerges such as a proposal to build a 600-megawatt coal-fired plant in an ecologically sensitive area, discourse sustains and reflects not only the everyday life situations of those directly and indirectly impacted, but visions they have about their futures that people really do not and probably cannot comprehend, from the perspectives of our everyday lives (Vincent 1980, Orrell 2007).

To describe these visions of the future, the glosses or words and phrases that people use to cover their interests need to be uncovered. And these glosses, when unpacked, become stories with constitute components and imagery. The purpose of a narrative analysis of this sort is to explicate the values that support ways of thinking about climate change and the future.

In the narratives of the different players in this coal plant drama, we discovered four tales of global warming. They are the environmental anti-coal story, the cost-benefit narration which is pro-business, the legal and regulatory procedures for plant approvals, and common public opinion themes.

Narrative analysis recognizes that storytelling is distinctively human, and that stories are composed of elements that are fairly consistent from story to story. As naturally occurring talk, a narrative carries within it personal experiences, themes of comedy, tragedy, and nuanced messages that may hide messages embedded within the organization of the narrative itself (Franzosi 1998). Labov suggests that narrative analysis is "one method of recapitulating past experience by matching a verbal sequence of clauses to the sequence of events which (it is inferred) actually occurred (Labov 1972, 359-60).

Some stories about the coal plant were formal presentations to the Arkansas Public Service Commission, others were found in letters to the editor of local newspapers, and most were just ordinary conversations. The stories contain what Fine calls "nature work" (Fine 1992). Fine (1998) proposes the term nature work to refer to the process by which people construct nature. Culture and nature are interactive phenomena; one cannot exist without the other. What constitutes nature at even given historical period results from the coming together of academic, scientific and everyday life meanings in concrete social networks. Mushroomers, in a sense, make their outdoor world from their knowledge and interests. We follow this conceptualization to show that talking and doing something about a coal plant is as much about people, their knowledge and interests, as it is about a world or externalized earth.

The Green Future Story

The green future story describes a triumph over tragedy. To reach this future, one must first see the tragedy of the present—a tragedy that started in the past during the Industrial Revolution.

There's a huge gap between the understanding of global warming by the relevant scientific community and that of those who need to lead the response and solve the problem: the policy-makers. And then there is the level of understanding of the general public. We've had, in the past thirty years, one degree Celsius of global warming. But there's another one degree Celsius in the pipeline due to gases that are already in the atmosphere. And there's another degree of temperature rise in the pipeline because of the energy infrastructure now in place—for example, power plants and vehicles that we're not going to take off the road, even if we decide that we're going to address this problem.

The Energy Department says that we're going to continue to put more and more CO_2 in the atmosphere each year—not just additional CO_2 but more than we put in the year before. If we do follow that path, *even for another ten years*, it guarantees that we will have dramatic climate changes that produce what I would call a different planet—one without sea ice in the Arctic; with worldwide, repeated coastal tragedies associated with storms and a continuously rising sea level; and with regional disruptions due to migration, freshwater shortages and shifting climatic zones. (Summarized from a talk delivered at the National Press Club by Dr. James Hansen, director of NASA's Goddard Institute for Space Studies (2007).)

At a press conference held on the step of the Arkansas State Capitol, Dina Nash, speaking for the Arkansas Sierra Club, also tells this version of the green story:

The group before you today represents the Arkansas Coalition for Clean Energy, a group of concerned citizens who want Arkansas to lead in the fight to keep our air clean for the health of our people and our planet. Hundreds of concerned scientists from every political party and country are telling the world that we must quickly shift from the burning of fossil fuels to other, cleaner energy sources. We join the following list of states which have said NO TO COAL ENERGY in recent months: Alaska, California, Colorado, North Carolina, Idaho, Texas, Illinois, Oregon, Florida, Nevada, Kansas, Oklahoma, and Washington. Contrary to the recent full page ads, coal energy is NOT clean energy. The Turk plant plans to spew over 6 million TONS of carbon dioxide gas per year for the average 40 year life expectancy of a coal plant (240 million tons, in all). Add to that sulfur dioxide and nitrous oxides, the mercury, and the radioactive particulate (tons), and we have a real mess in our air and water! That's the same amount as the amount of auto pollution from half the cars and light trucks on the road in Arkansas right now, which is a lot. Coal isn't clean." Next followed a plea from the Coalition for Clean Energy (various environmental organizations) for our Governor and his newly- appointed Global Warming Commission to study the air quality consequences before the Arkansas Department of Environmental Quality permits another huge coal plant. Our Coalition then described growing threats to life from the CO2 increases: more droughts, floods, pests, diseases, and loss of human life and wildlife. The speech told of the estimates of US premature deaths at over 60,000 people a year and how the human costs of putting over 240 million more tons of carbon dioxide in our air had not been thoroughly considered by our state's regulatory agencies. The speech concluded with three questions: "First, do we owe our lungs to the folks in Texas, Oklahoma, and Louisiana who want more electric power supply? And second, who will offer their child or parent to be first to have asthma so people in other states can have their lights on at night? And third, when will our Chambers of Commerce and business leaders get the message that we urgently need radical changes to our energy sources and more efficient energy from alternative energy and more efficient building and auto emission regulations?"(Speech delivered on the Capital steps, March 2008).

Personal meanings often accompany green stories. The motivations for telling the green story are rooted in experiences, beliefs, and values. My wife, Dina Nash, the activist, relates:

I first heard the topic of the earth's burning up long ago in Dr. Paul Shirra's Physical Science Class in 1964 at the University of Arkansas. When he told us the earth would probably burn up, even the rocks, and that we would all perish. Then he said Earth would turn into a cold, dark star with no life left on it... forever! At that time, he could only say this would happen several centuries in the future.

For decades, I tried to discuss this idea with many people, most of whom had never heard of this theory. I hoped he was wrong, because I love and trust the earth to take care of us if we take care of it. Then, in 1997, then President Will Clinton and Vice President Al Gore began worldwide caucusing about the earth-warming effects of greenhouse gasses, urging a global warming pact among all nations. Until then, my world seemed safe from stories about life-ending calamities except the Christian one about the imminent Second Coming of Christ and a reckoning for all sinners.

Mr. Gore continued to sound the alarm, resulting in the film, *Inconvenient Truth*, which began airing in 2007. In this film, Mr. Gore describes with some alarm the positive correlation between increasing fossil fuel usage and the increase in CO_2 in the atmosphere which raises the temperature of the earth. So not only is the sun going to turn into a fiery nova and burn itself and us up in the distant future, but we as a global population, could ruin the earth long before that. In fact, we could end up raising the surface temperature of the earth a few degrees by 2050, ruining the climate, killing millions of people, making Earth a living hell, and forcing the extinction of thousands more of species of plants and animals. Since 2007, we have read annual reports of the Intergovernmental Panel on Climate Change which publishes annual predictions of the possible scenarios for our weather and survival chances, which by now you probably know well.

In 2007, I was elected Vice President of the Central Arkansas chapter and was soon asked if I'd be the "point person" on a campaign to keep more coal plants from being built in Arkansas. After a public hearing conducted by ADEQ that we went to at Hope, Arkansas and two press conferences to raise awareness in the media, the Sierra Club was making a strong, visible stand against the coal plant. Unlike the hunt club coalition, Sierra Club was not allowed to be a legally sanctioned "intervenor" in the appeal of the Air Permit at ADEQ, because it had not filed its appeal during the 30 day period between Dec.1 and Dec. 31 of 2007, but we could speak against the coal plant anywhere we wanted to. At the public hearing in Hope, we learned that the SWEPCO officials in nice suits were silver-tongued and numerous, and that they had their public relations team working well. Every farmer in a cowboy hat and boots who stood to sell or haul dirt to build the platform for the plant, lay pipe for a pipeline, build a fence , lay cross ties for the rail bed that hauled the coal, or get paid for a wastewater drain line to go across their land showed up to speak for the coal plant. The Hope Chamber of Commerce sent their Mayor to say it would be good for their town, economically. Our cadre of four educated types from the capital city of Little Rock looked like "furiners", so it was instantly the locals against the "furiners". Each party got to talk two minutes to the group for public comment. A local doctor talked about lung disease and heart attacks from coal fumes; a female forester talked about PM2.5 levels in the forest (fine particulate) that will add to the haze that's already a problem there from other pollutant sources, and that a coal plant in the area will exceed the Federal PM2.5 particulate guidelines.

The points we made that night about the air and water pollution effects on people and wildlife were heavily reinforced by the lawyer for the cooperating hunting clubs from the area that would be most impacted by the pollution: the Hempstead County hunt club coalition. The land they owned was adjacent to the coal plant property and had been untouched by development for two generations, except for a few small cabins. The hunters were upset about the plume of pollution from the coal stacks because of impending nerve damage from mercury in their fish, ducks, and deer.

The Sierra Club stands for protection of the environment and public health, so we had two reasons to be there, standing against a dirty energy plant. SWEPCO speakers promoted the John W. Turk plant as being one using the currently cleanest technology and denied that there would be no more than a "golf-ball sized amount of mercury" emitted there over the life of the plant. (The official estimate was about 300 pounds of mercuric oxides emitted over a forty year period: some golf-ball!)

This began our efforts to contain the attempts by the Southwestern Electric Power Company staff to look and sound environmentally friendly and to paint them as they and their parent company are, nationwide. We knew their history of causing serious health problems and deaths in the Ohio River Valley and the East Coast, culminating in a huge judgement against them in the courts in 2008.

Citing the 2006 book by Jeff Goodell, *Big Coal*, we pointed out that the coal industry has also devastated mountaintops in West Virginia, Kentucky, and Tennessee, and that the streams below these coal mines get polluted and silted over, to the point that no one should eat the fish or drink the water, and the water creatures start showing genetic neurological mutations. IQs decrease in children in those areas, and birth defects are more frequent in babies.

At about this time, several things were happening inside and outside our organization. In January, Gene was asked by National Sierra, his bosses, to give a larger percentage of his time to the No to Coal campaign, since stopping coal plants had become a nationwide fight. As volunteers became more engaged, Gene became ambivalent about all the involvement, sensing a shift in the balance of power in his organization, taking back the point person role and becoming more involved, himself. Coal companies began placing full page ads in many newspapers (see example here) claiming coal to be clean power. Landowners in Arkansas who had shale on their land (the dirtiest low grade goal) formed a coalition and began promoting shale sales, which was very frightening in terms of health consequences. The Arkansas Governor decided not to pursue the idea of shale-burning at the Turk plant, after impacts from Sierra Club and others. More good news was that coal plants were rejected in many states, so that at first the number rejected was13, but that soon went to 48, nationwide, over about a three month period in late 2007. In this personal story, narrative themes crisscross. Devotion to green issues becomes palatable through commitment, friendship and public performance. The great cause of a green future gets tangled up in intimate relationships that claim turf and responsibility and mix formal and informal roles into a drama. While many such stories can be related as versions of the green narrative, this one illustrates the basic elements: 1) the imperative to overcome present actions at both the individual and collective level that are not sustainable and transition to a new way of life governed by norms of collective survival, 2) the transformation of tragedy to triumph, and 3) the emotional links to the narrative.

What the Public Thinks

The public does not literally talk and is not capable of concocting a story. However, we are quite comfortable with phrases such as "The public has spoken," or "the public is outraged or angry." Throughout history, publics have resisted political power and even rebelled. In our society, keeping up with the public voice is a full-time occupation for pollsters.

For several decades now, pollsters have been asking people what they think about global warming. The results are both expected and, depending on which way you talk about it, alarming. Since the topic first entered the national conversation, the public has become increasing aware of the problem. For example, when asked how well they understand global warming, there has been an increase from 53 percent to 74 percent of Americans who say they understand very or fairly well.

Still, this increased understanding, whatever it is, apparently does not do much to change how much people worry about the effects of climate change. The percentage saying they worry a fair amount or a great deal changed little from the 63 percent in 1989 when NASA's Dr. James Hanson first testified before Congress. In fact, it dropped to 62 percent in 2006 since a high of 72 percent in 2000, and it most recently is back up to 75 percent (Saad 2021).

Even though a slight majority of Americans worry very much about the effects, when asked about the magnitude of the effects if nothing is done to address global warming, over half (66 percent) anticipate the worst. As is often the case when attempting to understand public discourse, contradictions abound. How can so few Americans worry about the effects of global warming, yet so many say the effects, when they come, will be catastrophic? Since public opinion has no single speaker, no unitary cognitive process, we find puzzles that can confound us because we retell the story of public opinion according to how it makes sense to us.

There can be little question that the way people think about global warming is influenced by the way they think about other matters. The issue is highly partisan with 82 percent of Democrats saying the effects of climate change are already evident, while only 29 percent of Republicans think so. When asked about the urgency of this matter, again, those with Republican political identity seem far less convinced and far less troubled by the tragic narrative of global warming (Saad 2021).

In public discourse, economic and environmental concerns are often pitted against one another. The polls bear this out and show stark differences in which concerns win the hearts and minds of the public.

In 2006, the General Social Survey asked an array of questions about global warming, which mirror and supplement the Gallup poll data. The picture that emerges is only a bit out of focus. People know about warming of the earth; they generally believe that it is real and that it is influenced by human activity. They have little confidence in business leaders and even less in elected officials to act in way that might serve a collective good. The public expects there to be a scramble to preserve what one has, when things really heat up.

Why cite survey data? Because they give an estimate of what people might be thinking and doing about a specific issue such as the Turk coal plant. That is, if we can get a sense of a general dialogue going on in the public, we might be able to see these parameters of meanings working their way through the campaign. Stopping the coal plant may be seen by the people of the anti-coal campaign as necessary steps to mitigate the warming already going on, and as setting a precedent for the future. People in the public might wonder what is really going on and whose interests are being served.

Public opinion from a poll turns out to be a non-narrative; that is, it provides content but lacks the features of a naturally occurring story. It does not communicate character and emotional involvement; there are no heroes or villains in the structured questions that pollsters ask. However, the stories are implicit in the numbers, and they are of interest, reflecting values and beliefs about preserving ways of life. The public, it seems, sees plusses and minuses in the issues that surround global warming. Citizens who live around the proposed Turk plant heavily favor the coal plant. They do not see the tragedy in the story. To them, the story has a happy ending if local tax revenues and job numbers go up.

Stories of Legal Decisions

The Turk plant has operated now for nearly a decade with the approval of the Arkansas Department of Environmental Quality. SWEPCO purchased the land near the pristine swamp land long before starting the process to ask for approval from state regulatory agencies. They moved ahead with confidence and presumption of support from the local residents who anticipate an economic boom in their community.

Looking at legal issues surrounding the siting and permitting of a coal plant, a different narrative unfolds. It is a story of rights, regulations, and rule of law. This story is perhaps all too familiar. It starts with historical precedent and ends with setting a contemporary one. The precedence for taking minerals from the earth is deeply embedded in American law. Decisions generally follow a balancing act between protection of private property and the common good, often defined within the context of a community.

Making Sense: An Eco-Fable

Uncertainty about global warming can compound the difficulty in finding the political will to do anything about it (Orrell 2007, 311). And there is always the problem of validating predictions whenever human action can alter outcomes. This problematic is sometimes called the Nineveh problem. Scientific predictions are validated through observation. Predictions about the catastrophic effects of global warming are like prophesies of doom. If they are not heeded, then the impending catastrophe would make observational verification impossible or at least render it irrelevant to the tasks of coping with the consequences of human survival on a radically altered planet. If they are heeded, then the prediction never came true, and doubt about its validity can remain.

The Nineveh problem, as you might recall, gets its name from the biblical account of the prophet, Jonah. Here is a modern eco-fable, loosely fashioned on that Biblical passage. The Jews and the people of Nineveh were really not on the same page, especially on matters of ecology. Seems the Ninevites were a pleasure-loving, high-living lot. They had little regard for the carbon footprint they were producing. Many did not know what a carbon footprint might be. To them, their style of life was "non-negotiable." These Ninevites burned all sorts of materials to make possible their extravagant ways of living. They were even planning to build a giant plant that burns rocks and drill holes deep in the earth that would leave behind scars on the earth's surface and chemicals of unknown effects deep in the earth.

They did these things so that they could see through the night and drive their vehicles wherever they wished, whenever they wanted to. They had already built many such rock- burning plants and drilled many such holes in the ground, with little regard to what the consequences might be to the air they breathed and the food they ate. As long as they could choose and do as they pleased, the cycle of taking from the earth and using the earth continued. Such was their birthright, so the Ninevites believed.

To Jonah, the Ninevites were a loathsome lot. Jonah and his people tried to follow nature's laws as revealed to them through the Method of Knowing, which suggested that all things have limits and are part of the equilibria of nature. Jonah himself followed the green path. One day a scientist of highest regard spoke to Jonah, saying "You must warn the Ninevites of the conse-quences of their ways. You must tell them to comply with the laws of natural equilibria or suffer dire consequences, nigh to extinction." Jonah replied, "So be it. The nasty Ninevites deserve such a fate." This reply offended the Sci-entist and he retorted: "So your fate shall be sealed with theirs." Jonah was trapped in a belly so to speak. He thought about it for three days and nights and, then, replied to the high scientist, "You are correct. My fate is theirs. I shall go to Nineveh and predict to them their consequences based on solid science."

And so, Jonah prophesied climate change, ice melting, raising sea levels, the extinction of polar bears, and rapid changes in growing seasons. He drew out the logical conclusions of these things for the everyday life of the Ninev-ites. He made clear how necessity dictates sustainable habits of life, including changes in agriculture and especially in rock burning and hole drilling in the earth. He was eloquent, and he inspired others to prophesy.

There are many Jonahs today, and Ninevites, still intent on "non-nego-tiable" ways of living on earth. The original story ended with the people of Nineveh heeding the prophecy and thereby rendering it false. The present one, however, has just begun. Will we heed the prophesy of science and save contemporary Nineveh? Will more Jonahs be liberated from the bellies of whales? A historical footnote: What happened to the real Nineveh over the course of centuries? It is now an archeological site on bank of the Tigris River in the suburbs of the city of Mosul, Iraq. Perhaps smoke from burning oil wells and bombed out buildings wafts over the ancient ruins? Should histori-cal Nineveh's fate be part of the eco-fable?

CONCLUSIONS

Strategies for and against the coal plant in the narrow sense of the campaign and global warming in the broader sense reflect emerging images of the world as natural. The opposing images anchor feelings and decisions about the coal plant and expose a cognitive and an emotional connection between the lived experiences of actors in the exchange. Deconstructing this dialogue points toward changes in images instead of the scientific "facts" of the matter. Action is, therefore, directed at personal connections that can be made between everyday life experiences and images of the world as natural.

We can summarize the four narratives that we learned about through our activism as anti-coal, cost/benefits, legal procedural, and pubic opinion. Each narrative constructs a theme which has attributes. Anti-coal calls for limits on greenhouse gases, depicts hypothetical green economies, is new-urban and cosmopolitan in perspective, stressing the global interconnectedness or an ecological worldview. Implicit within the narrative are controls and regulation, but these are rarely given much detail. Cost/benefits stories are tales of who suffers and who benefits. Coal, hence the Turk plant, are portrayed as necessary for sustaining current life styles. No alternative vision of the future is developed as is the case with the anti-coal narration. Short-term rewards such as jobs and revenues for local communities trump an ecological perspective as the locals most likely to feel the impact of the plant believe that whatever harm the plants to nature is offset by the prospect of bringing local residents closer to prosperity and full participation in the American dream. The legal/procedural telling demands fluency in legal terminology. It is outside the vernaculars for everyday life, although terms such as "settlements," "claims," and "rulings" may become part of vernaculars. Zoning and protected areas, precedence and rule of law, state or regional legislative control act out the meanings for the people involved in the drama of the Turk plant. Finally, what the public thinks may serve as the background, a screen, for the stories to unfold. As people become more familiar with climate change and its consequences, their awareness of the how other people seem to understand the issue frames the meanings that the plant takes on. To the degree that these meanings reflect the polarized and conflictual character public opinion, the Turk plant becomes like a lightning rod for expressions of opinion. These four narratives are intertwined throughout our experiences in trying the stop the plant.

Personal experiences are at the core of each narrative. Whether people conflict, cooperate or simply ignore each another, the ways they apprehend what is taking place around them (the construction of the plant in their community) assume narrative forms. This is the nature-work of how people understood this massive construction project in southeastern Arkansas.

Chapter Eight

Personal and Public Sociology

At the end of this fragment of a memoir, this exhibition of translated personal experience into sociology, I want to make a case for the role that personal sociology can play in efforts to include sociological perspectives in public discourse.[1] How relating personal experiences can interject insights that readers might appreciate that they would not when these insights were expressed in conventional sociological writing. Ben Agger (2000) wielded a hatchet on the writing styles that characterize professional sociology calling them "secret." He meant that the style is so peculiar to the discipline that only the credentialed professional can understand and apply whatever valid or persuasive information might be contained within. Reviewing journal articles from the top publications, he takes apart the sections of a scholarly article, from abstract, review of literature, through methods to an adroit discussion of the use of mathematics as a kind of scientism that characterizes the professional writing style of contemporary sociology. As I read Agger, I was reminded of what a colleague once told me about sociologists' preoccupation with developing ever more sophisticated methods. He said, "Sociologists often use a butcher knife when a paring knife would do."

From Agger I learn that it is imperative to find a style for communicating important and even transformational information from sociological research to a broad audience, that is, to the public. He suggests that a public writing of sociology should 1) reveal the author; 2) engage in self-translation, that is, reveal assumptions and confess to intellectual and social interests; and 3) address major public issues, at least those that might influence policy and practice in a given society. Agger repeats that he is not lamenting the passing of the golden age of sociology because he thinks that the mathematization of discipline has deep roots that led to the scientism of today's journals, but he does cite authors whose ideas did become part of public discourse. Mills's

139

concept, the power elite, and recently "structural racism" are good examples. While a sociological insight, a finding, or a principle might become irrefutable as a part of the way journalists write and speak, instead, settled meanings for concepts among sociologists are used as political flash-points by some journalists. A few examples include how accurate descriptions of income inequality are often ignored, as is documentation of institutional racism, invidious status distinctions, and core concepts such as relative deprivation.

Can sociology reclaim or at least seek to defend and apply its findings and perspectives? Agger hopes so and believes that his critiques of the secret style can break through the training graduate students receive and encourage sociologists to write for the public. It is interesting to me that the magazine given that task by the American Sociological Association, *Contexts: Sociology for the Public*, has been at the task for 20 years with the guidance of many different editors. Before demonstrating that personal sociology can be a player in public sociology, let me provide a background for understanding efforts to make social science an important part of public discourse.

When I was in graduate school, *Psychology Today* magazine began its long and successful run as a conduit for the discipline of psychology to the general magazine-reading public. It didn't have advertising then. It presented the latest research and thinking about topics such as mental health and even social issues such as prejudice against minority groups. I recall we graduate students discussing why sociology didn't have such an outreach—why no *Sociology Today*? We attributed sociology's lack of public appeal to the critical stances that sociology took, explicitly or implicitly. *Psychology Today* had years of financial struggles, even being briefly (1983 to 1987) owned and managed by the American Psychological Association. But the editors stress positive and clinical approaches to helping people understand and even heal. Such an approach to understanding the human condition is consistent with core assumptions that support American individualism. Today the magazine has adapted to social media with blogs, links to therapists, and articles about celebrities. While not a peer-reviewed magazine, its advice reaches far and is regarded as relying on solid and verifiable sources for its articles and sections.

Sociologists did not ignore public outreach. In 1962 Irving Louis Horowitz started *Transaction*. I have a foggy memory of early issues of *Transaction* magazine which I recall as paper, almost like a comic book. The articles dealt with international matters and were often critical of US involvement. Today, that magazine has become *Society* (a professional journal) that continues to publish "the latest scholarship on the central questions of contemporary society." Eminent thinkers have published and continue to publish in the journal. For example, Amitai Etzioni has an article in the May 2021 issue about rethinking capitalism. Robert Merton, Levi-Strauss, William J. Wilson, and many others have contributed to the journal. *Society*, however, has a low impact score (.67, compared to 5.39 for the *American Sociological Review*). I wonder if Horowitz in the 1960s envisioned *Society* as a scholarly journal with a low profile and limited outreach.

While the professions of psychology and sociology reach out to a public audience, psychology has been more successful. And the American Sociological Association recognized that an effort needed to be made. Hence, the establishment of *Contexts: Sociology for the Public*. In its 2002 inaugural issue with a slightly different title (*Contexts: Understanding People in Their Social Worlds*), such contemporary topics as welfare reform, and poverty and language shift and maintenance are discussed and the newly recognized specialty of visual sociology made its appearance with Doug Harper's photographic essay on dairy farms. I mention Doug Harper because he was an undergraduate student of Jim Spradley's at Macalester College. Doug was so impressed by Spradley's *You Owe Yourself a Drunk* that after graduation he actually took to the rails photographing "tramps." He published *Good Company: A Tramp Life*, his first book, and a very compelling illustration of personal sociology.

Contexts has published some excellent issues that serve as examples of how sociologists address current events and conduct research that adds depth to our understanding of these issues. For example, the spring 2016 is devoted to "boundaries and unstable states" and includes summaries of current research on the limits of same-sex acceptance, parenting transgender children, and a moving story by Gary David about his personal sociological understanding of the diagnosis of an illness his newborn daughter had.

So, *Contexts* can work as public and personal sociology. Still, many articles are framed as important because important authors contributed them. There is still a disciplinary nod to how articles are written and how they introduced. The editors of the winter 2021 issue write

> Our Winter 2021 issue is a special issue edited by Victoria Reyes and Marco Garrido, two outstanding early-career scholars who are transforming how we understand urban life and global politics. This issue on ethnographies of the Global South promises to reveal more cutting-edge research on issues critical to our work as sociologists.

While I do not know the exact circulation numbers for the magazine, and I have a strong suspicion that most readers of *Contexts* are teachers of sociology and their students, so I am not sure how widespread the outreach of the magazine is. As a retired sociologist still actively writing and reading, I find *Contexts* an efficient way to "keep up with things." Sometimes I look for the sources of summarized articles, and, on occasion, I am inspired by an article, and I share it with colleagues and friends. I offer the following personal story of my effort to put the magazine to its test.

I am married to a wonderful woman named Dina (co-author of chapter Four) who comes from a very large and distinguished family. She has three sisters and a brother. By the time I joined the family, each sibling, except for the brother, was married with children, some of whom were adults. We moved to Little Rock to be close to Dina's mother who was in her eighties at the time and who lived to be two months shy of 100. She was a grand dame, presiding over large family occasions. (I referred to this family as a Malthusian nightmare.)

I read *Contexts* with regularity. I had just read Lane Kenworthy's "Tax Myths" (2009) when the subject of taxes was being discussed casually among several men. I mentioned his article that outlined how some of the common beliefs people have about how taxes function in a given economy are myths. My remark at first fell on deaf ears, but then Eddie, my brother-in-law and a successful businessman, now retired and once a mayor, challenged my rendition of Kenworthy's point that heavy taxation does not necessarily reduce economic competitiveness. He heard this as meaning that I might be in favor of raising taxes, which, of course, I was and still am.

In this staunchly conservative family (all except the reigning queen who was curiously liberal in beliefs about social issues and open to listening to unpopular ideas) taxes are evil and anti-business. I dropped the topic and a day or so later related this story to my wife who insisted that I should pursue the topic and perhaps even copy "Tax Myths" and give a copy to Eddie. At the next opportunity, I went armed with copies of "Tax Myths" and I rehearsed what I wanted to say, going over the charts in the article. The article discussed four myths: 1) that heavy taxation reduces economic competitiveness, 2) that republicans favor tax cuts because they believe they are good for the economy and key constituents, 3) that taxes reduce inequality, and 4) that globalization makes heavy taxation impossible.

Kenworthy's points about these myths are demonstrated with charts that demand some close attention. Here's what I communicated about his analysis to Eddie. First, conventional economic textbooks regard taxes as a necessary drag on economies. But this is misleading because of the way the health of economies is assessed (by their Gross National Product). Instead, a more suitable indicator, competitiveness, is required. This indicator includes infrastructure, macro-economic policy, health and primary education, higher education and training, market efficiency, technological readiness, business sophistication, and innovation. A scattergram shows no relationship between heavy taxes (as a percent of GNP) and competitiveness. The United States and Switzerland have relative low taxation and high competitiveness, while Denmark and Sweden have high taxes and high competitiveness.

For myth number two, Kenworthy traces the rise of the Republican belief that tax cuts stimulate the economy, and he concludes that Republicans are united about the value of tax cuts. However, this is not the primary reason they advocate for less taxation. Instead, they are riding a wave of anti-tax sentiment that has swept the country since the 1970s. The relationship between taxes and inequality (myth number three) is best expressed as "Taxes are quite important for inequality reduction, but what matters most is their quantity rather than their progressivity " (2009, 30). Tax revenues are positively related to reductions in the GINI index for western nations as are transfers of wealth.

Finally, myth number four: that globalization makes heavy taxation impossible. Acknowledging that nations have felt pressure to keep taxes low in order to compete with nations with cheap and abundant labor, this seems to have not resulted in a "race to the bottom."

> [There has] been little change in tax revenues as a share of GDP . . . tax revenue levels in 1989 and 2007 in 20 nations (both years are business cycle peaks, so it's fair to compare them). In a few countries tax revenues decreased, but in others they increased. In most they stayed more or less the same. (Kenworthy 2009, 32)

Now, how did I fare? I had hoped to at least open Eddie's mind to a more sophisticated and comparative way to think about taxes. Eddie and I had a comfortable relationship. I did not challenge his conservatism and he pretty much ignored me whenever conversations turned to politics or even sociological analysis. Needless to say, my little foray into macroeconomics failed. He listened politely and then changed the topic to something in daily life we could talk about. In the interest of a convivial familial atmosphere, we never talked about taxes again.

When I was a graduate student, my thesis advisor gave some advice which I have sometimes heeded. He said, talk about important issues and topics only with friends. I know what he meant. That before you get into details and nuances of a topic, you have to feel comfortable talking; that is, you assume that no matter what you say, within the limits of the friendship, you will not be the target of abuse, or attempts to place you in categories that you don't want to be a member of. For example, that you think like a stale Marxist, your reasoning is sophomoric or just plan stupid. Friends listen and offer gentle criticism, or the banter is framed as cordial.

I think Habermas's theory of communicative competency adds some credence to the advice. While the theory is richly complex, it starts with a concept of normal communication, that is, an assumption of symmetrical background knowledge. The assumptions that underlie conversations are that what one party knows, feels, and does, is accessible to the other. Within the domain of friendship, there is a degree of accessibility to background knowledge and emotions. One friend can understand the other. When this is not the case, distorted communication occurs, and asymmetrical conversational footings give an advantage to one speaker over the other.

Back to Eddie. We were related because our wives were sisters. I like Eddie, but I knew we shared very little in common about our life views, or our understandings of political and economic worlds. When I look back on my feeble attempt at converting a conservative, I realize that my approach was too scholarly. I was asking him to consider some detail, and I introduced enough confusion so that he reverted to his familiar ideology for security. I was just one of those liberal professors and, therefore, what I had to say was either of no worth or downright dangerous. Because Eddie and I were brothers-in-laws, and we valued convivial encounters when were together, we both chose to follow the path of least resistance which meant keeping our opinions and, in my case, a modicum of expertise under wraps.

Here's how I understand what happened to the rapprochement. We learned decades ago from the brilliant work of Harvey Sacks (see Silverman 1998) that people give and create meaning to interactions through categorization. Sacks called the process of using categories membership categorization devices (MCDs). He demonstrated the concept of MCD by using an ambiguous utterance (THE BABY CRIED THE MOMMA PICKED IT UP). This utterance, when spoken without vocal intonation can be heard as having three meanings, that the baby is the mother's and she (the mother) picked it up, that the baby can speak and cries out "the momma picked it up," or that the mother exclaims that the baby picked it up. This was more than word play or semantics: it demonstrated how human cognition works by imposing categories on what is said or happens to make meanings clear. Chomsky (1957) followed a similar approach of using ambiguous sentences to show that languages have deep structures. More recently cognitive scientists like George Lakoff (2009) have referred this way to hear meaning as framing. Also, Goffman worked toward this same insight in his book, *Frame Analysis: As Essay on the Organization of Experience* (1974).

For Eddie, this theorizing simply meant he and I couldn't communicate, or construct a mutual footing for understanding because we use fundamentally different ways of organizing our cognitions and social worlds. *Pathways* magazine carried an article several years ago that succinctly presents the beliefs that function to create meanings for conservatives and liberal on issues of poverty and inequality. Conservatives see taxes as a burden, a drag on free markets, and hence a harm to the economy. Liberals see taxes a tool that governments have to generally do good, that is, establish safety nets, protect the population, and lessen suffering.

To Eddie, Kenworthy must have been seen as a liberal even though the purpose of his article was clearly nonpartisan and analytic. No need to confess that I wanted to penetrate Eddie's beliefs about taxes. At the face-to-face level, maybe my thesis advisor was right: only get serious about a topic with friends, and friends are different from kin.

But what's to be done? Personal sociology requires a comment to sociological perspectives and to demonstrating the link between analysis and personal experience. Recently, I decided that in retirement, to make sociology more publicly accessible, I would write opinion editorials for our local newspaper. Thanks to the openness to my work on the part of the opinion editors of the *Democrat/Gazette*, the state's largest newspaper, and I have published several op-ed pieces. I include some of them here to 1) give them a wider exposure than just to Arkansans and 2) demonstrate how I have tried to incorporate sociological ideas and perspectives into editorials in an effort to show the value of personal sociology in public discourse.

"ONE MORE REASON WHY WE CAN'T AGREE" *DEMOCRAT/GAZETTE,* JULY 2018

Attitudes about issues and problems that have profound consequences for society and culture are polarized in ways public opinion pollsters have rarely seen. Among the best examples is the way opinions have become polarized about climate change. Gallup Poll director Frank Newport interviewed experts who explain this polarization as the result of partisan politics, changes in news media, and the influence that political elites have on loyalists' attitudes. I want to suggest another reason: the dramatic changes that have occurred in what counts as legitimate knowledge.

Institutions of higher education were founded, in some cases over 200 years ago, on a belief that knowledge could further the public good. Historically, Americans believed that life could be better for all through public and private investment in higher education. Not only were universities supposed to arbitrate through scientific research and archived knowledge, they were to recommend best practices where applicable. Ideally, institutions of higher learning were to serve as objective, or at least, impartial purveyors of knowledge and practices.

Life-changing discoveries and new ways of knowing about the world and the universe have their origins in research and teaching at institutions of higher learning. However, when trust in public institutions declines, as is the case today, alternative organizations emerge to produce knowledge and information that serves the specific interests of particular groups, businesses, or corporations.

These new purveyors of "knowledge" are often called think tanks or institutes. Some are affiliated with universities, but most are not. They go by names such as the Tax Foundation, Heritage Foundation, and the CATO and Heartland Institutes. These organizations have proliferated over the past decades, until today they challenge and even supplant some roles that universities once played. The findings of their research may serve the interests of a sponsoring organization and support particular public opinions, but often they do not meet the standard for peer reviewed, impartial knowledge and policy. Often, research results follow the money that funded the study in these institutes.

A handy way to assess the validity of any study, in addition to the usual methods of scientific and critical thinking, is to look at the goals and missions of the organizations that conduct the studies. For example, the Tax Foundation, which has actually been around since the great depression, now has on its board of directors some representatives from Price-Water-House-Cooper, Microsoft, Pepsi Co, and Eli Lilly. It advocates for "good tax policy [that] promotes economic growth by focusing on raising revenue in the least distortive manner possible," which usually means advocating on behalf of business endeavors. The Heritage Foundation promotes "public policies based on the principles of free enterprise, limited government, individual freedom, traditional American values, and a strong national defense." Heartland Institute's mission is to "discover, develop, and promote free-market solutions to social and economic problems." To these ends, the Heartland Institute convenes a yearly conference on Global Warming with the expressed intent to discredit the evidence that climate is changing, and in particular, that human activity has anything to do with it. In fact, they maintain a web site that posts papers refuting every conclusion of the United Nation's report on climate change, even touting the benefits of increased CO2 to human life. These conferences invite politicians and scientists who often cheer denunciations of "conventional" science. The Heartland Institute supports existing "free-market" solutions to climate change by denying that a political solution is necessary.

The mission statements of institutions of higher education read very differently, often with words and phrases such as the common good, creativity, opening minds and enacting core values such as integrity, inquiry, service, and public affairs.

Universities and colleges are true institutions. Think tanks and institutes are pseudo institutions, that is, they do not function as taken-for-granted arbitrators of knowledge. In a society with declining or loss of trust in core institutions, they are often cited and even have become part of "balanced" presentations in news, and in the Trump administration, in the formulation of government policies.

These well-funded research organizations, each with its insular interests, have professional spokespersons for their research and their interpretations of empirical research. For example, it is not difficult to identify the agenda that the Heritage Foundation espouses when its senior fellows interpret tax legislation, income distribution, or, say, the US prison system. My point is not to rail against these organizations or to suggest they should not exist, or even deny that they might align themselves with findings from the scientific community on a specific issue. It is to raise a red flag on behalf of the public good that they have managed to assume equal footing with universities and professional associations of scientists, thereby eroding the legitimate role that established universities heretofore played.

Universities still contribute to knowledge and evidence-based decisions made by businesses and governments, but their legitimacy has been challenged, and to compete, they too may distort their foundational values; that is, play the role of "debater" against the pseudo institutions.

Jurgen Habermas (a German sociologist) suggests that Western societies are experiencing a "legitimation crisis." And this crisis is one reason that ordinary citizens cannot seem to agree even on consensual scientific findings such as the causes of climate change. According to the concept, a "crisis" exists whenever an institutional structure of society, such as higher education, no longer has the authority to control or govern its domain. Authority depends, in large measure, on the taken-for-granted trust that citizens have in their institutions. Universities or professional associations are, then, in crisis whenever their research and their interpretations are so challenged that they become impotent.

Institutions of higher learning assumed legitimate authority through a long and complicated process that spans at least two centuries and culminated in science and technology that allow our modern way of life The values of honesty, impartiality, and the unfettered pursuit of truth served as the foundation for institutional legitimation. Today we face global problems that may be cataclysmic, and at the very least demand collective solutions. As long as these problems have partisan interpretations supported by institutes with special interests, legitimate collective solutions will be difficult, if not impossible, to achieve. Too many experts from too many think tanks may well be one more reason we can't agree.

"ALL MY THINGS AT THE CURB"
ARKANSAS DEMOCRAT-GAZETTE, DECEMBER 2018

Mathew Desmond, author of the Pulitzer Prize-winning book *Evicted: Poverty and Profit in the American City*, recently gave a talk at University of

Arkansas at Little Rock, thanks to the sponsorship of the Winthrop Rock-efeller Distinguished Lecture Series. A professor at Princeton, his book is about the practice of evicting people from their residences. He spoke about the emotions and hardships of being evicted, and he gave detailed and personal accounts of evictions from a variety of perspectives—the evicted and the evicting.

I sat in the audience impressed with his presentation. Not only did he ground his remarks in his two-year experience living among the evicted, but his newly founded Eviction Lab at Princeton provided a national context for an appreciation of the scope and seriousness of the problem for those who experience it and those who profit from it.

In our own city, the sight of household belongings stacked at the curb is common in low-income neighborhoods. Desmond relates how this happens. In one example, he documents the consequences of Wisconsin Works, a policy which requires able-bodied recipients to work for assistance. This program and others like it often have unintended consequences which can exacerbate the problems that they are supposed to solve. Wisconsin Works failed to discriminate between those able to work and those with emotional and behavioral disorders who fail at employment and end up evicted and homeless. And, profiteers who sell lists of the names of people who have been evicted to landlords with a similar effect as that of "the mark of a felon." Landlords refuse to rent to those with a past eviction, just as employers shun felons.

Desmond writes on the Eviction Lab website that "most poor renting families spend at least half of their income on housing costs, with one in four of those families spending over 70 percent of their income just on rent and utilities." Wages for poor families, particularly families headed by a single mother, have been nearly flat for several decades, while rents have risen. Furthermore, only one in four low-income families qualifies for affordable housing programs. After paying the rent, there is not enough money to budget or spend wisely.

Desmond's conclusion is that eviction drives those who experience it deeper into a cycle of hopelessness and homelessness. Poor families are often just one major car repair, medical expense, or run-in with the law away from disaster. Then, Desmond discussed ways to ameliorate and even eliminate the necessity for evictions. His proposal focuses on expanding rent subsidies. While political will would be required to enact his proposal of more comprehensive aid for paying rent, his analysis left his audience informed and hopeful that political solutions might be forthcoming.

What a jolt to compare Desmond's approach to what we just witnessed in the last midterm elections. I could not help but compare his description of evictions as a social problem to how similar problems are discussed in the political arena. Candidates from both major parties relied on emotional and rhetorical appeals for votes. How much different our political campaigns would be if politicians would run for office by detailing actual facts, trends, and interpretations of issues. Instead, they run elections that assume that voters are either incapable or unwilling to understand the complexities of problems in contemporary society.

While we are not surprised to learn that politicians believe that elections can only be won by persuading voters with emotional appeals, it might be time to try another approach. Instead of politicking with emotional appeal and ideological rhetoric wouldn't it be a wondrous change to have politicians and political parties campaign on evidence and informed understandings of issues like poverty and the role that evictions play in that depressing cycle of "for want of a nail the horse was lost." Likewise, our elected officials should be more open to detailed letters from their constituents. Now, political action groups encourage letter writers to state a position briefly. While we are wishing for change, how about television pundits and news organizations providing information on issues as thorough as Desmond's on eviction.

Professor Desmond reminds us that the social sciences can contribute to public discourse by describing the nature of social problems. Carefully documented understandings of a particular social problem and how that problem connects to economic and social forces can inspire searches for solutions. Evictions, the professor tells us, are part of a larger problem of poverty and profit in American cities. Evictions do not solve the problems of poverty, nor do they insure the value of rental property. Instead, they worsen poverty and contribute to the decline of property value.

While there are many solutions for keeping people's belongings off the curb, acting to solve or lessen the consequences of that problem often, if not always, has political implications. Voter and candidate should understand issues in their social and economic contexts. While voters have obligations, so do candidates. We should demand that they inform us, not just appeal to us. Professor Desmond's impassioned book on evictions can serve as a model.

"ELECTION LESSONS FROM 2020"
DEMOCRAT-GAZETTE, DECEMBER 2020

While every election cycle teaches us something about the American people and our system of government, 2020 is especially instructive. It seemed interminable, confusing, and it probably will have lingering effects. While the coronavirus pandemic had its impact on the election, there are permanent conditions that shaped how the election unfolded. Here are some lessons I suggest we should learn from the election cycle many of us would like to forget.

First, our elections last too long and are too expensive. This is not just a matter of never-ending breaking news or of misspent capital. During the long battle between two political philosophies, each side has the opportunity to hear thousands of repeated campaign messages. Repetition not only establishes memory ascendence, it can alter decision-making as well. While not the only reason for the polarization, the sheer repetition of messages conditions us to react emotionally to news and political discourse. The more repetition, the more likely emotional reactions crowd out the possibility of rational discourse. These emotional reactions range from fear or anger to boredom and provide scant opportunity for energetic and engaged discussion, researching possible social costs of promoted policies, polite disagreements, or negotiated compromises based on the common good.

A legally defined campaign season, during which contenders who have sufficient percentages of support in public opinion have government-funded access to public media, might more likely provide such opportunities. Political campaigns on social media outlets should also be confined to the election season. Whatever shape the final reform might take, it should concentrate official campaigning into a restricted season. This is a fairly common practice among modern democratic nations. The US campaign season is the longest and most expensive by nearly three times compared to other representative governments, and there is no law to prohibit it from becoming even longer and more expensive.

Second, our system needs to be more democratic. This is because a system that excludes some and favors others can create a detached and alienated citizenry with little confidence in all things governmental. From bottom to top, our government, both national and state, is designed to be unrepresentative of the actual distribution of political thought and feelings in a given constituency. Our winnter-take-all system deprives losers of voice and power. For example, in Arkansas, on any given political belief such as a women's right to a legal abortion, gun control, election reform, and so on, a majority of Arkansas may believe one way, but our representatives to Washington, another. In the last election, 35 percent of the presidential votes from Arkansas went to Biden, yet all six of our electoral votes (100 percent) went to Trump. If you are consistently liberal in your politics and you live in Arkansas, you have no voice in Washington, DC. From all appearances, our representatives to DC ignore voters of the minority party for six to four years, depending on their office. We do a disservice to the electorate by suggesting that we live in a democracy. Compared to other democratic nations, the United States ranks twenty-first in how representative we are, and we are close to being declared a "failed democracy " by the Economist Intelligent Unit (a research group of the Economist Group).

Our system raises expectations and the inevitable disappointment that comes from watching one's candidate lose or watching him or her deal with the consequences of victory. While imperfect, a system that is organized upon the principle of proportional representation encourages diversity and negotiated government policy, not my side or theirs. In our system, hopes are so high and disappointments are so dramatic, due to the fact that losing may mean you're out of the game for several years. In a proportional system such as a parliamentary one, you are still in the game with your membership in parliament.

Of course, transforming our system from a representative republic, which was designed to guard against democracy, into a system that reflects the composition of the constituency would require a constitutional convention that might be so contentious as to be dysfunctional. Still, there is no shortage of suggestions about how to make us a more democratic nation. At the top of the list are these: eliminating the electoral college, reforming how legislative districts are defined (banning gerrymandering), term-limiting Supreme Court Justices, passing a new voting rights act that encourages higher voter turnout and makes barriers to vote illegal, ending the filibuster, eliminating "dark" money, granting statehood to Washington, DC, and Puerto Rico, and lowering the voting age to 16. Ironic that a battle cry of the American revolution was "no taxation without representation," yet today 14 million legal residents (green card holders) pay payroll, property, and sales taxes, sometimes for years, yet cannot vote or collect Social Security.

Third, make our political system less cumbersome and more agile. Our political system functions slowly and deliberatively, and this often creates stalemates. Our government appears uncaring to many voters. For environmentalists, watching the ineffective and even counter-productive policies and practices that favor the fossil fuel industry can led to cynicism and resignation. Our government is designed to be inefficient. I learned this in civics class with Mr. Hamn at Roosevelt Junior High in Tulsa. He explained how the three branches of government guard against rash and ill-conceived legislation. Mr. Hamn taught us that while our system of checks and balances is supposed to promote rational decision making, it makes quick responses to emergencies difficult and adaptations to social change laborious.

Since WWII, presidents have used emergency powers to circumvent Congress's war authority and generally accomplish what they think should be done. This is partially the result of the inertia and dysfunction that is built into the US governing system. To the citizenry, careful deliberation may provoke frustration and polarization. For example, Senate Majority Leader Mitch McConnell recently said there is no need to craft a coronavirus stimulus plan that the President will refuse to sign: but what about the citizens' needs? Wouldn't it make more sense to have economists and other social science use their objective analyses to arrive at budget that would meet the needs of the unemployed and homeless working poor and of the overall economy? Instead, we have a stalemate based on differing ideological perspectives about the proper role of government.

Perhaps rule changes in both houses could expedite the passing of bills and curb the power of committees to kill legislation that has popular support. Forcing votes in the Senate on measures passed in the House of Representatives might also untangle stalemates. A dysfunctional government does little to make legitimate whatever laws it passes and to inspire confidence in our system that would encourage informed voting.

Understanding the reasons that the 2020 election was so worrisome for many citizens is not just a matter of the personalities of those running for office, but the consequence of the nature of our republic, the pressing need for campaign reform, and the need to re-examine what kind of representative government we might need to prepare for difficult future challenges.

So, this ends the journey of personal sociology. I have displayed my interests, my predilections, and my aspirations. I remain bullish on sociology and I am motivated by what a colleague at Missouri State University once told me. He said that he awoke each morning with a motto in his head: "Stamp out ignorance in the Ozarks." I fear there is much more stamping to do within and outside the Ozarks.

NOTES

1. Parts of this chapter were previously published in the *Arkansas Democrat-Gazette* and are used with permission.

Bibliography

Adams, Tony E., Ellis, Carolyn and Jones, Stacy Holman 2017. "Autoethnography," in *The International Encyclopedia of Communication Research*. Christine S. Davis and Robert F. Potter (Associate Editors). New York: John Wiley & Sons, Inc.

Agar, Michael. H. 1996. *The Professional Stranger: An Informal Introduction to Ethnography* New York: Academic Press.

Agger, Ben, 2000. *Public Sociology: From Social Facts to Literary Acts*. New York: Rowman and Littlefield.

Allen-Collinson, J. And H. Owton. 2015. "Intense Embodiment: Senses of Heat in Women's Running and Boxing." *Body and Society* 21 (2): 245–268.

Alter, Joseph S. 1993. "The Body of One Color: Indian Wrestling: the Indian State and Utopian Somatics." *Cultural Anthropology* Vol. (February): 49–72.

Anderson, Edward. 2009. *Inclusive Masculinity: The Changing Nature of Masculinities*. New York: Routledge.

Anderson, Elijah. 2011. *The Cosmopolitan Canopy: Race and Civility in Everyday Life*. New York: W.W. Norton and Company.

Anderson, Leon. 2006. Analytic Autoethnography. *Journal of Contemporary Ethnography* 35 (4): 373–395.

Arluke, Arnold, Louanne Kennedy, and Ronald C. Kessler. 1979. "Reexamining the Sick-Role Concept: An Empirical Assessment." *Journal of Health and Social Behavior* 20 (1): 30–36.

Atkinson, Michael. 2008. "Exploring Male Femininity in the Crisis: Men and Cosmetic Surgery." *Body and Society* 14: 67–87.

Averill, Gage. 2003. *Four Parts, No Waiting: A Social History of American Barbershop Harmony*. New York: Oxford University Press.

Bauman, Zygmunt. 2000. *Liquid Modernity*. New York: Policy Press.

2005. *Liquid Life*. Malden. MA: Polity Press.

Beasley, Christina. 2008. "Rethinking Hegemonic Masculinity in a Globalizing World." *Men & Masculinities* 11 (1): 86–103.

Becker, Howard S. 1953. "Becoming a Marihuana User." *American Journal of Sociology*. 59: 235–242.

———. 2017. *Evidence.* Chicago, IL: University of Chicago Press.

Berger, Peter L. 2014. *Redeeming Laughter: The Comic Dimension of Human Experience* (2nd Ed.). Boston: De Grutter.

Berger, Peter. 1963. *Invitation to Sociology: A Humanistic Perspective.* Garden City: Doubleday.

Bettocchi, Arlo, et.al. 2009. "Patient and Partner Satisfaction after AMS Inflatable Penile Prosthesis Implant." *Journal of Sexual Medicine* 7: 304–309.

Bingham, Shawn Chandler and Alexander A. Hernandez, 2009. "Laughing Matters: The Comedian as Social Observer, Teacher and Conduit of the Sociological Perspective." *Teaching Sociology* 37: 335–352.

Blau, Judith. 1988. Music as Social Circumstance. *Social Forces* 66 (4): 883–902.

Bloomer, Herbert. 1969. *Symbolic Interactionism: Perspective and Method.* New Jersey: Prentice-Hall.

Bochner, Arthur and Carolyn Ellis. 2016. *Evocative Autoethnograph.* New York: Rutledge.

Boston Common. No date. Back in Dad and, Mother's Day, Sheet Music 2M73 Nashville, TN: Barbershop Harmony Society.

Bourdieu, Pierre. 1984. *Distinction: A Social Critique of the Judgment of Taste.* Cambridge: Harvard University Press.

Brain, Marshall. 2017. "How Laughter Works." HowStuffWorks.https://science.howstuffworks.com/life/inside-the-mind/emotions/laughter.htm.

Capek, Stella M. 1999. "Community: Institutional Failures and the Demise of Carver Terrace." *Research in Social Problems and Public Policy.* (Volume 7): 139–162. JAI Press.

———. 1993. "The Environmental Justice Frame: A Conceptual Discussion and an Application." *Social Problems* 40 (1): 5–2

———. 1992. "Environmental Justice, Regulation, and the Local Community." *International Journal of Health Services* 22 (4): 729–746.

Carvalheira, Ana, Rita Santana, and Nuno M. Pereira. 2015. "Why Are Men Satisfied or Dissatisfied with Penile Implants? A Mixed Method Study on Satisfaction with Penile Prosthesis Implantation." *Journal of Sex Medicine* 12:2474–2480.

Chin, Richard. 2011. "The Science of Sarcasm? Yeah Right." Smithsonian.com.

Chomsky, Noam. 1957. *Syntactic Structures.* The Hague: Mouton and Co.

Chorus Impact Study. 2009. *How Children, Adults, and Communities Benefit from Choruses.* Washington DC: Chorus America.

Coleman, James S. 1993. "The Rational Reconstruction of Society." *American Sociological Review* 58 (February): 1–15.

Colyer, Corey J. 2015. "W.I. Thomas and the Forgotten Four Wishes: A Case Study in the Sociology of Ideas." *American Sociologist* 46: 248–268.

Connell, Raewyn W. 2005. *Masculinities.* Berkeley: University of California Press.

Connell, Raewyn W., and James E. Messerschmidt. 2005. "Hegemonic Masculinity: Rethinking the Concept." *Gender and Society* Vol 19. No. 6: 829–859.

Conrad, Peter. 1992. "Medicalization and Social Control," *Annual Review of Sociology* 18: 209–232.

———. 2005. "The Shifting Engines of Medicalization." *Journal of Health and Social Behavior* 46: 3–14.

Conrad, Peter and Michael Schneider. 1992. *Deviance and Medicalization: From Badness to Sickness.* Philadelphia: Temple University Press.

Cooky, Cheryl, and Michael A. Messner. 2018. *No Slam Dunk: Gender, Sport, and the Unevenness of Social Change.* New Brunswick, NJ: Rutgers University Press.

Cooley, Charles H. 1922. *Human Nature and the Social Order.* New York: Charles Scribner and Sons.

Copes, Heith and Andy Hochstetler. 2003. "Situational Construction of Masculinity among Male Street Thieves." *Journal of Contemporary Ethnography* 32 (June): 279–305.

Critchley, Simon, 2002. *Humour.* New York: Routledge.

Curry, Timothy Jon. 1993. "A Little Pain Never Hurt Anyone: Athletic Career Socialization and the Normalization of Sports Injury." *Symbolic Interaction,* Vol. 16 (Fall): 273–290.

Darling, Rosalyn Benjamin and Peter Stein (eds). 2017. *Journeys in Sociology: From First Encounters to Fulfilling Retirements.* Philadelphia: Temple University Press.

Davidson, Jane W. 2006. "Men in Chorus: Collaboration and Competition in Homosocial Behavior." *Psychology of Music,* Vol. 34 (No. 2): 219–237.

Davis, Fred 1992. *Fashion, Culture and Identity.* Chicago: University of Chicago Press.

———. 1979. *Yearning for Yesterday: A Sociology of Nostalgia.* New York: Free Press.

Davis, Murray S. 1993. *What's So Funny: The Comedic Conception of Society and Culture.* Chicago: University of Chicago Press.

De Andrade, Daniela Dorneles. 2010. "On Norms and Bodies: Findings from Field Research on Cosmetic Surgery in Rio de Janeiro Brazil." *Reproductive Health Matters.* Vol. 18: 74–83.

Delaney, Tim. 2006. *Seinology: The Sociology of Seinfeld.* New York: Prometheus Books.

Desmond, Matthew. 2016. *Evicted: Poverty and Profit and the American City.* New York: Crown Publishers.

Dieser, Rodney B. 2008. "Tales from Grades 1 through 12: Understanding the Complex Web of Multiple Life Forces Located in Schools." *The Alberta Journal of Educational Research* 54 (3): 292–308.

Dodsworth, Laura, 2017. *Manhood: The Bare Reality.* London: Pinter and Martin.

Donovan, Brian. 1998. "Political Consequences of Private Authority: Promise Keepers and the Transformation of Hegemonic Masculinity." *Theory and Society* 27: 817–43.

Duggan, Mark, and Steven D. Levitt, 2002. "Winning Isn't Everything: Corruption in Sumo Wrestling." *The American Economic Review,* Vol. 92 (December): 1594–1605.

Elias, Norbert. 1982. *Power and Civility.* New York: Pantheon.

Elridge, John, 2001. *Wild Heart: Discovering the Secrets of a Man's Heart.* Nashville: Nelson Books.

Emerson, Joan P. 1970. "Behavior in Private Places: Sustaining Definitions of Reality in Gynecological Examinations," in *Recent Sociology* No. 2 Hans Peter Dreitzel. New York: The Macmillan Company. 74–97.

Erikson, Kai T. 1976. *Everything in Its Path: Destruction of Community in the Buffalo Creek Flood*. New York: Simon and Schuster.

Faulkner, Robert. and Jane W. Davidson. 2006. "Men in Chorus: Collaboration and Competition in Homo-Social Behavior." *Psychology of Music* 34 (No. 2): 219–237.

Festiner, Leon, Henry W. Riecken, and Stanley Schachter, 1956. *When Prophesy Fails*. Minneapolis MN: University of Minnesota Press.

Findlay, Heather. 1992. "Freud's "Fetishism" and the Lesbian Dildo Debates." *Feminist Studies* 18: 563–579.

Fine, Gary Alan. 1998. *Morel Tales: The Culture of Mushrooming*. Cambridge: Harvard University Press.

———. 1992. "Wild Life: Authenticity and the Human Experience of 'Natural' Places," in Carolyn Ellis and Michael G. Flaherty (eds.) *Investigating Subjectivity: Research and Lived Experience*. Newbury Park, California: Sage Publications. 156–175.

———. 1987. *With the Boys: Little League Baseball and Preadolescent Culture*. Chicago: University Chicago Press.

Flaherty, Michael. 2001. "Present, Past, and Future: Conjugating George Herbert Mead's Perspective of Time." *Time and Society* 10:147–61.

Foster Bellamy John, Brett Clark, and Richard York, 2010. *The Ecological Rift: Capitalism's War on the Earth*. New York: Monthly Review Press.

FrankTalk.org. 2017. https://www.franktalk.org/.

———. 2018. https://www.franktalk.org/.2018. https://www.franktalk.org/.

Franklin, Clyde. 1989. *Men and Society* Chicago: Nelson-Hall.

Franzosi, Roberto. 1998 "Narrative Analysis—Or Why (And How) Sociologists Should be Interested in Narrative." *Annual Review of Sociology*, Vol. 24: 517–554.

Friedman, David M. 2001. *A Mind of Its Own: A Cultural History of the Penis*. New York: Free Press.

Fromkin, Victoria and Robert Rodman. 2003. *Introduction to Language*. Orlando, FL: Harcourt and Brace College Publishing.

Gallagher, Sally K., and Carol Smith. 1999. "Symbolic Traditionalism and Pragmatic Egalitarianism." *Gender and Society* 13: 211–233.

Gallagher, Sally K., and Sabrine L. Wood. 2005. "Godly Manhood Going Wild?: Transformations in Conservative Protestant Masculinity." *Sociology of Religion* 66: 135–159.

Gallup, George. "Gender Gap in Support for Animal Rights, but No Significant Generational Differences." Survey. In The Gallup Poll: Public Opinion 2003, 170–71. Wilmington, DE: Scholarly Resources Inc., 2004.

Gans, Herbert, 1979. "Symbolic Ethnicity: The Future of Ethnic Groups and Cultures in America." *Ethnic and Racial Studies* 2: 1–20.

Garfinkel, Harold and Anne Warfield Rawls. 2002. *Ethnomethodology's Program: Working Out Durkheim's Aphorism*. New York: Rowman and Littlefield.

Garnett, Liz. 1999. "Ethics and Aesthetics: The Social Theory of Barbershop Harmony." *Popular Music*, Vol. 18 (January): 41–61.

General Social Survey. "GSS General Social Survey." NORC. Norc at the University of Chicago. Accessed January 6, 2022. https://gss.norc.org/.

Gilmore, David D. 1990. *Manhood in the Making*. New Haven: Yale University Press.

Goffman, Alice, 2014. *On the Run: Fugitive Life in an American City*. Chicago: University of Chicago Press.

Goffman, Irvine. 1963. *Stigma: Notes on the Management of Spoiled Identity*. New York: Simon and Schuster.

———. 1959. *The Presentation of Self in Everyday Life*. Garden City: Doubleday Anchor.

———. 1974. *Frame Analysis: As Essay on the Organization of Experience*. Cambridge, Massachusetts: Harvard University Press.

———. 1981. *Forms of Talk*. Philadelphia: University of Philadelphia Press.

Goodell, Jeff. 2006. *Big Coal: The Dirty Secret Behind America's Energy Future*. New York: Houghton Mifflin Company.

Gray, Herman. 1995. *Watching Race: Television and the Struggle for "Blackness"*. Minneapolis, MN: University of Minnesota Press.

Grain, David. 2003. *Blue Chicago: The Search for Authenticity in Urban Blues Clubs*. Chicago: University of Chicago Press.

Grossberg, Lawrence 1992. *We Gotta Get out of This Place: Conservatism and Postmodern Culture*. New York: Routledge.

Guerrero, Ed. 1993. *Framing Blackness: The African American Image in Film*. Philadelphia, PA: Temple University Press.

Guttentag, Marica and Paul Secord. 1983. *Too Many Women: The Sex Ratio Question*. Beverly Hills: Sage Publications Inc.

Habermas, Jurgen. 1970. "Towards a Theory of Communicative Competency," in Hans Peter Dreizel (ed.) *Recent Sociology*, New York: Macmillan.

Haiman, John. 1998. *Talk is Cheap: Sarcasm, Alienation and the Evolution of Language*. New York: Oxford University Press.

Hamamoto, Darrell Y. 1989. *Nervous Laughter: Television Comedy and Liberal Democratic Ideology*. New York: Praeger.

Hanson, Dian (ed,). 2012. *The Little Book of Big Breasts*. Cologne: Taschen Books.

———. (ed.), 2013 *The Little Book of Butts*. Cologne: Taschen Books.

Hansen, James, 2003. "Can We Defuse the Global Warming Time Bomb?" Downloaded from Wikipedia, May 2008.

———. "Global Warming: Connecting the Dots from Causes to Solutions." Lecture. National Press Club and American University. Washington, D.C. February 2007. http://www.columbia.edu/~jeh1/2007/Dots_20070226.pdf.

Harrison, Peter. 1992. "Descartes on Animals." *The Philosophical Quarterly*, Vol. 42, No. 167. (Apr): 219–227.

HBO.com. 2006. Home Box Office. 4 June 2006. https://www.hbo.com.

Heath, Melanie. 2003. "Soft-Boiled Masculinity: Renegotiating Gender and Racial Ideologies in the Promise Keeper's Movement." *Gender and Society* 17: 423–444.

Henninger S, C Höhn, C Leiber and MM Berner. 2015. "Treatment Expectations of Men with ED and Their Partners: An Exploratory Qualitative Study Based on Grounded Theory." *International Journal of Impotence Research* 27: 167–172.

Henry, Jim. 2001. Historical Roots of Barbershop Harmony. *The Harmonizer* July/ August: 13–17.

Higgins, Paul. 2004. How was School Today? *A Father and Daughter's School-Year Journey*. New York. Hamilton Books.

Higgins, Paul C., and John M. Johnson (eds) 1988. *Personal Sociology*. New York: Praeger.

Himmelstein, Jerome L. 1986. "The Social Basis of Antifeminism." *Journal for the Scientific Study of Religion* 25 (1): 1–15.

Hodgson, Dorothy L. 1999. "Once Intrepid Warriors: Modernity and the Production of Maasai Masculinities." *Ethnology* 38 (Spring): 121–150

Humphreys, Laud, 1970. *Tearoom Trade: Sex in Public Places*. Piscataway, New Jersey: Transaction Publisher.

Hunt, Darnell M. (ed.) 2005. *Channeling Blackness: Studies on Television and Race in America*. New York: Oxford University Press.

Hynes, Eugene, 1989. "To See Yourselves as Others See Us: Using Humor to Teach Sociology." *Teaching Sociology* 17: 476–479.

Inglehart, Ronald. 1997. *Modernity and Postmodernity: Cultural, Political and Economic Change in 43 Societies*. Princeton, New Jersey: Princeton University Press.

Irvine, Leslie. 1999. *Codependent Forevermore: The Invention of Self in a Twelve Step Group*. Chicago: University of Chicago Press.

———. 2004. "A Model of Animal Selfhood: Expanding Interactionist Possibilities." *Symbolic Interaction*. 27 (1): 3–21.

———. 2017. "Wild Selves: A Symbolic Interactionist Perspective on Species, Minds and Nature," in Bradley H. Brewster and Antony J. Puddephatt (eds.) *Microsociological Perspectives for Environmental Sociology*. New York: Routledge. 128–142.

Irwin, John. 1977. *Scenes*. Beverly Hills, CA: Sage Publications.

Jamison, Wesley V., and William M. Lunch. 1992. "Rights of Animals, Perceptions of Science, and Political Activism: Profile of American Animal Rights Activists." *Science, Technology, & Human Values*, Vol. 17, No. 4, (Autumn): 438-458

Jasper, James M. and Dorothy Nelkin.1991. *The Animal Rights Crusade: The Growth of a Moral Protest*. New York: Free Press.

Jerolmack, Colin. 2003. "Tracing the Profile of Animal Right Supports: A Preliminary Investigation." *Society and Animals* 11 (3): 245–263.

Jones, Kathrine W. 2001. "I've Called' Em Tom-ah-toes All My Life I'm Not Going to Change." Maintaining Linguistic Control over English Identity." *Social Forces* 79 (3): 1060-1094.

Kalmijn, Matthijs. 1991. "Shifting Boundaries: Trends in Religious and Educational Homogamy." *American Sociological Review* 56: 786-800.

Kaplan, Danny. 2007. "Folk Models of Dyadic Male Bonds in Israeli Culture." *The Sociological Quarterly* 48 (Winter): 47–72.

Kenworthy, Lane. 2009. "Tax Myths." *Contexts* 8 (3): 28–32.

Kimmel, Michael. 2006. *Manhood in America: A Cultural History*. New York: Oxford.

———. 2008. *Guyland: The Perilous World Where Boys Become Men*. New York: Harper Collins Publishers.

Kleinman, Sherryl, and Martha Copp. 1993. *Emotions and Fieldwork*. Newbury Park, CA: Sage Publications.

Klinkner, Philip A. and Rogers M. Smith. 1999. *The Unsteady March: The Rise and Decline of Racial Equality in America*. Chicago, IL: The University of Chicago Press.

Kozol, Jonathan. 2005. *The Shame of the Nation: The Restoration of Apartheid Schooling in America*. New York: Random House.

Krishnan, Vidya. "Severed Penis Sewn Back." Hindustan Times. Hindustan Times, December 10, 2006. https://www.hindustantimes.com/india/severed-penis-sewn -back/story-UrwFtjoVl8FzCxSVcxGkWJ.html.

Labov, William. 1972. *Sociolinguistic Patterns*. Philadelphia: University of Pennsylvania Press.

Lakoff, George. 2009. *The Political Mind: A Cognitive Scientist's Guide to Your Brain and Its Politics*. New York: Penguin Books.

Lakoff, George and Mark Johnson. 1980. *Metaphors We Live By*. Chicago: University of Chicago Press.

Lazarsfeld, Paul and Merton, Robert K. 1948. "Mass Communication, Popular Taste and Organized Social Action." Lawrence Bryson (ed.). *Communication of Ideas*. New York: Harper. 95–118.

Leyser, Ophra. 2003. "Doing Masculinity in a Mental Hospital." *Journal of Contemporary Ethnography* 32: 336–359.

Lipsitz, George. 1986. "The Meaning of Memory: Family, Class and Ethnicity in Early Network Television Programs." *Cultural Anthropology*. Vol. 1. No.4: 355–387.

Lovell, Terry. 2000. "Thinking Feminism with and against Bourdieu." *Feminist Theory* 1 (1): 11–32.

Lugosi, Peter. 2006. "Between Overt and Covert Research Concealment and Disclosure in an Ethnographic Study of Commercial Hospitality." *Qualitative Inquiry* 12 (3): 541–561.

Luker, Kristin. 1984. *Abortion and the Politics of Motherhood*. Berkeley, CA: University of California Press.

Manderson, Lenore and Lesley Stirling. 2007. "The Absent Breast: Speaking of the Mastectomied Body." *Feminism and Psychology*, Vol. 17 (1): 75–92.

Marshall, Brent K., and J. Steven Picou. 2008. "Postnormal Science, Precautionary Principle, and Worst Cases: The Challenge of Twenty-First Century Catastrophes." *Sociological Inquiry*, Vol. 78 (May): 230–247.

Martin, Rod. 2007. *The Psychology of Humor*. Elsevier, 2007.

McGraw, Peter, and Joel Warner, 2014. *The Humor Code*. New York: Simon and Schuster.

McNall, Scott. 2011. *Rapid Climate Change: Causes, Consequences and Solutions*. New York: Routledge.

McPherson, Miller, Lynn Smith-Lovin, and Matthew E. Brashears. 2006 "Social Isolation in America: Changes in Core Discussion Networks over Two Decades." *American Sociological Review* Vol. 71 (June): 353–373.

Mead, George H. (ed. C. W. Morris). 1934. *Mind, Self and Society*. Chicago: University of Chicago Press.

Mead, George Herbert. 1932. *The Philosophy of the Present*. Chicago: University of Chicago Press.

Merton, Robert K Jr. 1957. *Social Theory and Social Structure: Revised and Enlarged Edition*. Glencoe: The Free Press.

Messner, Michael. 1989. Review of Fine, Gary Allen, *With the Boy: Little League Baseball and Preadolescent Culture*, in *Gender and Society*, Vol. 3 (March): 139–140.

———. 1990. "Boyhood, Organized Sports and the Construction of Masculinities." *Journal of Contemporary Ethnography* 18, No. 4: 416–444.

———. 1993. "Changing Men and Feminist Politics in the United States." *Theory & Society* 22: 723–737.

———. 2002. *Taking the Field: Women, Men, and Sports*. Minneapolis, MN: University of Minnesota Press.

Messner, Michael A., and D. F. Sabo (eds.) 1990. *Sport, Men, and the Gender Order: Critical Feminist Perspectives*. Champaign, Ill.: Human Kinetics Books.

Messner, Michael, and Jeffrey Montez de Oca. 2005 "The Male Consumer as Loser: Beer and Liquor Ads in Mega Sports Media Events." *Signs: Journal of Women in Culture and Society*, Vol. 30 (no. 3): 1879–1909.

Miller, Toby 1995. "A Short History of the Penis." *Social Text*. No. 43: 1–26.

Murphy, Robert, 1987. *The Body Silent*. New York: Norton.

Nadel, Alan. 2005. *Television in Black-and-White: Race and National Identity*. Lawrence, Kansas: University of Kansas Press.

Nash, Jeffrey E. 1980. "Weekend Racing: Understanding the Accomplishment of Well Being." *Urban Life: A Journal of Ethnographic Research* 8 (July): 199–217.

———. 1989. "What's in a Face: The Social Character of the English Bulldog." *Qualitative Sociology* 12 (Winter): 357–370.

———. 2012. "Ringing the Chord: Sentimentality and Nostalgia among Male Singers." *Journal of Contemporary Ethnography* 41: 581–606.

Nash, Jeffrey E., and Eric Lerner. 1981 "Learning from the Pros: Violence in Youth Hockey." *Youth and Society*, Vol. 13 (December): 229–244.

Nash, Jeffrey E., and David P. McCurdy 1990. "Cultural Knowledge and Systems of Knowing." *Sociological Inquiry*, Vol. 59 (2): 117–126.

Nash, Jeffrey E., and Dina Nash. 2016. "Feminizing a Musical Form: Women's Participation as Barbershop Singers." in Christopher J. Scheider and Joseph A. Kotarba (eds.) *Symbolic Interactionist Takes on Music*. Howard House, UK: Emerald Press.

Ogles, Richard H. 1980. "Concept Formation in Sociology: Observational Data by Observational Concepts." Lee Freese (ed.). *Theoretical Methods in Sociology: Seven Essays*. Pittsburgh, Pa. University of Pittsburgh Press. 143–174.

Oldenburg, Raymond. 1999. *The Great Good Place*. New York: Paragon House.

Opler, Marvin K. 1945. "A 'Sumo' Tournament at Tule Lake Center." *American Anthropologist*, Vol. 47 (January-March): 134–139.

Orrell, David. 2007. *The Future of Everything: The Science of Prediction.* New York: Thunder's Mouth Press.

Paley, Maggie, 1999. *The Book of the Penis.* New Youk: Grove Press.

Parsons, Talcott. 1951. *The Social System.* Glencoe, IL: The Free Press.

Peek, Charles W. Nancy J. Bell; Charlotte C. Dunham. "Gender, Gender Ideology, and Animal Rights Advocacy." *Gender and Society,* Vol. 10, No. 4. (Aug., 1996): 464–478.

Perry, Brea L. 2011. "The Labeling Paradox: Stigma, the Sick Role, and Social Networks in Mental Illness." *Journal of Health and Social Behavior,* Vol. 52: 460–477.

Peterson, Richard A., 1997. *Creating Country Music: Fabricating Authenticity.* Chicago: University of Chicago Press.

Pielke, Roger A. Jr. and Richard T. Conant, 2003. "Best Practices in Prediction for Decision-Making: Lessons from the Atmospheric and Earth Sciences." *Ecology* 84 (June): 1351–1358.

Prause, Nicole, et al. 2015. "Women's Preferences for Penis Size: A New Research Method Using Selection among 3D Models." *PLOS*: 1 (September): 1–17.

Putnam, Robert D. 2000. *Bowling Alone: The Collapse and Revival of American Community.* New York: Simon and Schuster.

———. 2007. "E Pluribus Unum: Diversity and Community in the Twenty-First Century." *Scandinavian Political Studies* 30 (2): 137–174.

Rankin, Katherine, et al. 2009. "Detecting Sarcasm from Paralinguistic Cues: Anatomic and Cognitive Correlates in Neurodegenerative Disease." *Neuroimage* 47: 2005–2015.

Riem, Christa Hoffman. 1994. http:/www.ssoar.info/ssoar/bitstream/handle/document/1035/ssoar-1994-hoffman-riem-elementare_phanomeme_der_lebenssituation.pdf.

Riemer, Jeffrey W. 1977. "Varieties of Opportunistic Research." *Urban Life* 5:467–477.

Rocchio, Vincent R. 2000. *Reel Racism: Confronting Hollywood's Construction of Afro-American Culture.* Boulder, CO: Westview Press.

Rooker, Steven A, et al, 2019. "The Rise of the Neophallus: A Systematic Review of Penile Prosthetic Outcomes and Complications in Gender-Affirming Surgery." *Journal of Sexual Medicine*: 1–12.

Rosa, Alfred F., and Paul A. Eschholz. 1974. "Bunkerisms: Archie's Suppository Remarks in *All in the Family.*" Paul. A. Eschholz, Alfred. E. Rosa, and Victor P. Clark (eds.). *Language Awareness.* New York: St. Martin's Press. 183–189.

Ross, Catherine E., and John Mirowsky. 1984. "Men Who Cry." *Social Psychological Quarterly* 47 (2): 138–147.

Roth, Julius A. 1963. *Timetables.* Indianapolis: Bobbs-Merrill.

Rotundo, E. Anthony. 1993. *American Manhood: Transformation in Masculinity from the Revolution to the Modern Era.* New York: Basic Books.

Roy, Donald. 1952. "Quota Restriction and Goldbricking in a Machine Shop." *American Journal* of Sociology 57: 425–42.

Saad, Lydia. "Global Warming Attitudes Frozen since 2016." Gallup.com. Gallup, April 5, 2021. https://news.gallup.com/poll/343025/global-warming-attitudes-frozen-2016.aspx.

Sacks, Harvey. 1974. "An Analysis of the Course of a Joke's Telling in Conversation," in R. Bauman and J.F. Sherzer (eds.) *Explorations in the Ethnography of Speaking.* Cambridge, UK: Cambridge University Press. 337–353.

———. 1975. "Everyone Has to Lie." In B. Blount and M. Sanches (Eds.), *Sociocultural Dimensions of Language Use.* New York: Academic Press. 57–80.

Sanders, Clinton. 2008. *Customizing the Body: The Art and Culture of Tattooing.* Philadelphia: Temple University Press.

Shai, Katherine. "What You Don't Know About Being A Female Wrestler." *Athlete Network,* September 29, 2017. https://an.athletenetwork.com/blog/what-you-dont-know-about-being-a-female-wrestler.

Scheff, Thomas J. 1997. *Emotions, The Social Bond, and Human Reality.* Cambridge: Cambridge University Press.

Schutz, Alfred. 1971. "Making Music Together: A Study in Social Relationship." *Collected Papers II: Studies in Social Theory.* The Hague: Martinus Nijhoff.

Schwalbe, Michael. 1996. "The Mirrors in Men's Faces." *Journal of Contemporary Ethnography* 25: 58–82.

———. 1996. *Unlocking the Iron Cage: The Men's Movement, Gender Politics, and American Culture.* New York: Oxford University Press.

Seeman, Melvin. 1959. "On the Meaning of Alienation." *American Sociological Review* 24: 783–791.

Seizer, Susan 2011. "On the Uses of Obscenity in Live Stand-Up Comedy." *Anthropological Quarterly.* 84: 209–234

Sheller, Mimi. 2007. "Bodies, Cybercars, and the Mundane Incorporation of Automated Mobilities." *Social and Cultural Geography* 8 (2): 175–197.

Sherif, Mauzafer. 1954. *Experimental Study of Positive and Negative Intergroup Attitudes between Experimentally Produced Groups: Robbers Cave Study.* Norman, OK: University of Oklahoma Press.

Silverman, David. 1998. *Harvey Sacks: Social Science and Conversational Analysis.* New York: Oxford University Press.

Smart, Ben. "While Erectile Dysfunction Increases, Use of Penile Implants Declines." CNN. CNN, June 23, 2015. https://www.cnn.com/2015/06/23/health/penile-implants-erectile-dysfunction/index.html.

Spradley, James P. 1980. *Participant Observation.* New York: Holt: Rinehart and Winston.

Stebbins, Robert A. 1976. "Music among Friends: The Social Networks of Amateur Musicians." *International Review of Sociology* 12: 12–73.

———. 1982 "Serious Leisure: A Conceptual Statement." *Pacific Sociological Review* 25: 251–272.

———. 1996. *The Barbershop Singer: Inside the Social World of a Musical Hobby.* Toronto: University of Toronto Press.

———. 2007. *Serious Leisure: A Perspective for Our Time.* New Brunswick NJ: Transaction.

———. 2009. *Personal Decisions in the Public Square: Beyond Problem Solving into a Positive Sociology.* New Brunswick NJ: Transaction.

Stein, Arlene. 2005. "Make Room for Daddy: Anxious Masculinity and Emergent Homophobias in Neopatriarchal Politics." *Gender and Society* 19: 601–620.

Stempel, Carl. 2006. "Moral Capital, and Support for the U.S. Invasion of Iraq." *Journal of Sport & Social Issues,* Vol. 30, Issue 1: 79–106.

Stephens, Elizabeth. 2007. "The Spectacularized Penis." Men and Masculinities.10: 85–98

Sutherland, Anne and Jeffrey E Nash. 1994. "Animal Rights as a New Environmental Cosmology," *Qualitative Sociology* 17 (2) Summer: 171–186

Swidler, Ann. 1986. "Culture in Action: Symbols and Strategies." *American Sociological Review* 51: 273–286.

Tamney, Joseph B, Stephen D. Johnson, Ronald Burton. 1992. "The Abortion Controversy: Conflicting Beliefs and Values in American Society." *Journal for the Scientific Study of Religion* 31, (1): 32–46.

Tawa, Nicholas E. 1995. "Songs of the Early Nineteenth Century, Part 1: Early Songs lyrics and Coping with Life." *American Music* 13 (Spring): 1–26.

Theberge, Nancy. 2003. "'No Fear Comes'" Adolescent Girls, Ice Hockey and the Embodiment of Gender." *Youth and Society* 34 (June): 497–516.

Tiefer, Leonore. 1994. "The Medicalization of Impotence: Normalizing Phallocentrism." *Gender and Society* 8: 363–77.

Tomasi, Luigi. 2000. *Emile Durkheim's Contribution to the Sociological Explanation of Suicide.* New York: Routledge.

Ucko, Peter L. 1969. "Penis Sheaths: A Comparative Study." *Proceeding of the Royal Anthropological Institute of Great Britain and Ireland.* 1969: 24–67.

User losangeles, post to "Saga of a Penile Implant," from FrankTalk.org, January 9, 2013, 8:10 p.m., https://www.franktalk.org/phpBB3/viewtopic.php?t=2506.

Van Den Hoonaard, Will C. 2011. *The Seduction of Ethics: Transforming the Social Sciences.* Toronto, Canada: University of Toronto Press.

Vannini, Peter and Dennis Waskul. 2006. Symbolic Interaction as Music: The Esthetic Constitution of Meaning, Self and Society. *Symbolic Interaction* 24 (1): 5–18.

Vasconcelos, Erika Franca de Souza. 2011. "I Can See You": An Autoethnography of My Teacher-Student Self. *The Qualitative Report* 16 (2): 415–440.

Veale, David, et al. 2014. "Am I Normal? A Systematic Review and Construction of Nomograms for Flaccid and Erect Penis Length and Circumference in up to 15,521 Men." *Sexual Medicine* 115: 978–986.

Vera, Hernan and Gordon, Andrew M. 2003. *Screen Saviors: Hollywood Fictions of Whiteness.* New York: Rowman, Littlefield.

Villarreal, Humberto and LeRoy Jones. 2012. "Outcomes of and Satisfaction with the Inflatable Penile Prosthesis in the Elderly Male." *Advances in Urology.* 2012. Article ID 240963 doi:10.1155/2012/240963.

Vincent, Jack E. 1980. "Scientific Prediction versus Crystal Ball Gazing: Can the Unknown Be Known?" *International Studies Quarterly,* Vol. 24, No. 3, (Sept): 450–454.

Wacquant, L. J.D. 1992. "The Social Logic of Boxing in Black Chicago: Toward a Sociology of Pugilism," *Sociology of Sport Journal*, 9 (September): 221–254.
———. 2004. *Body and Soul: Notebooks of an Apprentice Boxer*. Oxford: Oxford University Press.
———. "A Concise Genealogy and Anatomy of Habitus." *The Sociological Review* 64: 64–72.
Walker, Karen. 1994. "Men, Women and Friendship: What They Say, What They Do." *Gender and Society*. Vol. 8 (June): 246–265.
Wasko, Janet (ed.). 2005. *A Companion to Television*. Oxford: Blackwell Publishing
Waskul, Dennis and Phillip Vannini (Eds.). 2006. *Body/Embodiment: Symbolic Interaction and the Sociology of the Body*. Burlington, VT: Ashgate Publishing Company.
Weber, Max, 1946. *From Max Weber: Essays in Sociology* (eds. Gerth, H. H. And C. Wright Mills) New York: Oxford University Press.
Weigert, Andrew J. 1997. *Self, Interaction, and Natural Environment: Refocusing Our Eyesight*. Albany, New York: State University of New York Press.
Weinberg, Martin S. and Colin J. Williams. 2010. "Bare Bodies: Nudity, Gender, and the Looking Glass Body." *Sociological Forum* 25: 47–67.
Weinberg, Morten and Colin J. Williams. 2005. "Fecal Matters: Habitus, Embodiment and Deviance." *Social Problems* 52 (3): 315–336.
West, Mark D. 1997. "Legal rules and Social Norms in Japan's Secret World of Sumo." *The Journal of Legal Studies*. Vol. 26 (January): 165–201.
Williams, Robin M Jr. 1970. *American Society: A Sociological Interpretation*. New York: Knopf.
Wilson, Janelle L. 2005. *Nostalgia: Sanctuary of Meaning*. Lewisburg, PA: Bucknell University Press.
Wilson, William J. 2012/(1978). *The Declining Significance of Race: Blacks and Changing American Institutions*. Chicago: The University of Chicago Press.
———. (2012/ 1987) *The Truly Disadvantaged. The Inner City, The Underclass and Public Policy*. Chicago: University of Chicago Press.
———. 2009. *More Than Just Race: Being Black and Poor in the Inner City*. New York: W. W. Norton and Company.

Index

About the Author

Jeffrey E. Nash is professor emeritus (Missouri State University) and former chair of the Department of Sociology and Anthropology at the University of Arkansas at Little Rock. He also served as professor of sociology at Macalester College, St. Paul, Minnesota. He is author of *Deafness in Society* with Anedith Nash, *The Meanings of Social Interaction* with James Calonico, and he co-edited with Paul Higgins two editions of *Understanding Deafness Socially*. He has articles and book chapters on a wide range of topics from bulldogs to barbershop singing. With Charles Edgley, he is currently co-editor of *The Journal of Contemporary Ethnography*.